DIVORCE
AND THE
FAMILY BUSINESS

SECOND EDITION

DIVORCE
AND THE
FAMILY BUSINESS

SECOND EDITION

Editors:

Michael Drake,
Solicitor, Collyer-Bristow

Tim Lawrence,
Chartered Accountant

 **Family Law**

'1

Published by Family Law
a publishing imprint of
Jordan Publishing Limited
21 St Thomas Street
Bristol BS1 6JS

British Library Cataloguing-in-Publication Data

A catalogue record for this book is available
from the British Library.

ISBN 0 85308 646 X

Photoset by Mendip Communications Ltd, Frome, Somerset
Printed in Great Britain by MPG Books Ltd, Bodmin, Cornwall

PREFACE

In the preface to the first edition of this book we mentioned that the project had involved a challenging and thoroughly enjoyable collaboration between us and our respective firms. The second edition has proved equally challenging and similarly enjoyable.

We also said that the practice of family law was undergoing a very considerable change, citing the Family Law Act 1996, the various pilot schemes, the Woolf Report, recent and proposed changes in pension law, and the growth of mediation.

Again, all this still applies. The last three years have seen very significant developments in family law including in particular the shelving of the divorce reforms in the Family Law Act 1996, the development of the new Family Proceedings Rules, and the pre-action protocol, the introduction of pension sharing, dramatic changes to the child support regime, and a number of very important practice directions on case preparation. Inevitably there have also been a number of significant cases, not least the well-publicised case of *White*.

In this edition we have tried to set our advice against the background of these developments, and to reflect the changes in approach which the new Rules have introduced.

May we again reiterate our thanks to the Solicitors Family Law Association for permitting us to reproduce its guide *Good Practice in Family Law on Disclosure*. Thanks are also due to the partners and staff of PricewaterhouseCoopers for their assistance in updating the taxation and accounting content. Finally, our thanks to our publishers for their guidance and, yet again, their patience.

Michael Drake, Collyer-Bristow
Tim Lawrence
May 2001

CONTENTS

TABLE OF CASES

References are to paragraph numbers, Roman numerals are to introduction page number, references in *italic* are to Appendix page numbers.

TABLE OF STATUTES

References are to paragraph numbers, references in *italic* are to Appendix page numbers.

TABLE OF STATUTORY INSTRUMENTS

References are to paragraph numbers, references in *italic* are to Appendix page numbers.

TABLE OF ABBREVIATIONS

CPR 1998	Civil Procedure Rules 1998
FDR	family dispute resolution
FPR 1991	Family Proceedings Rules 1991
PPR	principal private residence
the new Rules	Family Proceedings (Amendment No 2) Rules 1999

INTRODUCTION

The purpose of this book is to address the problems which uniquely arise in divorce cases where there is a family business.

By combining the experience of solicitors and accountants, the book offers comprehensive guidance and advice which will alert practitioners in both professions, and other experts, to all the problems which can arise, and give a clearer understanding of the requirements of the court, and the most effective methods of meeting those requirements.

Over the last few years, the judges of the Family Division and the district judges throughout the country have consistently expressed concern at the manner in which costs levels have exploded, and at the seriously detrimental effect that this can have upon the families involved in matrimonial litigation. They have said so plainly and have made punitive costs orders and wasted costs orders. Many of their observations and the guidelines they have provided will be found throughout the book.

One major cause of this dramatic and judicially deplored increase in costs has been the extension of the process of discovery and investigation in ancillary relief applications. Another cause has been the inevitable uncertainty which arises in predicting the outcome of such applications, because of the discretionary nature of the jurisdiction, and the varying approaches adopted by the courts. The new Family Proceedings Rules (Family Proceedings (Amendment No 2) Rules 1999) do much to reduce the expansion of the discovery process, by placing the control far more firmly in the hands of the court; however, the underlying difficulties remain, and matrimonial litigation continues to be an extremely expensive and time-consuming exercise.

Most practitioners do their best to assess the likely outcome of an application accurately and realistically and work towards a satisfactory compromise. The difficulty of predicting the mood and decision of the court, in a case with unusual or especially complex features, is an inherent feature of the family jurisdiction. The process of identifying clear trends in judicial thinking is fascinating if not always rewarding, but it has become an increasingly necessary process in order to attempt to anticipate the court's decision and avoid confrontation.

The resolution of most applications is a two-stage process.

First comes the exercise of gathering the information and ascertaining the facts and figures; sometimes this is a co-operative and painless process for both sides, but all too frequently it is not.

Secondly comes the task of applying the criteria set out in s 25 of the Matrimonial Causes Act 1973 (see the Appendix) – whether in negotiation or ultimately at a hearing – to achieve a just and equitable conclusion.

Both the legal and accountancy professions have been faced with a serious dilemma. They must be seen to avoid confrontation and the accumulation of unnecessary costs wherever possible, and face criticism and possibly punitive costs orders against their clients or even their firms if they fail to make the correct judgment. At the same time, they must investigate the financial position thoroughly, professionally and comprehensively if they are to protect their client's interests, and in order to remove, or at least reduce, the risk that doubt will be cast upon their professional competence after the event, if, as their client perceives it, the exercise is unsuccessful.

This dilemma exists throughout the preparation of ancillary relief applications, in relation to many of the issues that arise in the course of disclosure. Nowhere is it more apparent than in the context of evaluating interests in businesses and companies, and the many and varied benefits in cash and kind, that can flow from them.

The dilemma has of course existed for many years, but, to the growing concern of the courts, there is now added the increased pressure on the level of professional fees, which are monitored and challenged by clients and opponents more readily than ever before. The new Rules include far more punitive provisions in relation to costs, increasing the pressure on practitioners to settle sensibly and early.

Thus the professional advisers must balance their duty to do competent work and to seek a financial benefit for their client against possible concern over accumulating fees which may be expressed by the client (and perhaps by other advisers in the team), whilst always bearing in mind the concerns of the judge if the case reaches court.

These concerns have now been reflected in the new Family Proceedings Rules incorporating the new procedure (initially operating as the Ancillary Relief Pilot Scheme) and involving far greater case management by district judges and judges from the outset. The process of establishing a timetable for exchange of Forms E, questionnaires and Statements of Issues; fixing a date for the First Appointment immediately upon the issue of the application; increasing judicial control over the disclosure of information; and incorporating a financial dispute resolution (FDR) hearing in the procedure, appears to be contributing to a higher level of settled cases. However, it is also accepted by practitioners that the costs under this procedure have become increasingly 'front loaded', in that the preparation of the Form E and all the accompanying paperwork; the attendances at court on the First Appointment and FDR, in each case with clients; and the exchanges of proposals throughout that period, require a more significant level of legal guidance and involvement than before.

The benefit appears to be that a greater percentage of cases are settling prior to the final hearing which is, of course, the most expensive exercise of all.

Against this background there is a move towards the more economical use of expert evidence, in particular at court, and increasingly a preference for the use of a single, jointly appointed expert, where appropriate. This has been reflected in the civil justice system, following the Woolf Reforms, and the approach is beginning to move to the family jurisdiction, with increased emphasis on the appointment of a single expert wherever it is practicable.

The debate still continues over the wisdom and effectiveness of a single joint expert accountant, appointed for example to value the family company, and at this stage it is far from clear how the approach of the courts will develop.

There is no doubt that the forensic accountant, appointed on behalf of one party, may have at least two, quite distinct, roles. The first will be to investigate the financial position of the other spouse, identifying the avenues of enquiry and the documentation that may be needed, considering and analysing it and advising. The second and subsequent role may be to offer a professional opinion on the value of business under investigation.

The first role is inevitably somewhat partisan, although it must of course be conducted under the guidance of the court and in a thoroughly proper and professional way. The second role requires a clear professional 'neutrality'; the responsibility of the accountant is to the court and not to the client.

For the client, it is often difficult to distinguish between the two roles. To date, it has generally not been necessary to do so, in the sense that the accountant retains the ultimate responsibility to stand back from the client, to give a professional opinion to the court and to explain and justify that opinion if called upon to do so. It remains to be seen how the accountant's role is to develop in the future and how rapid the move will be towards the regular appointment of a single joint expert.

This dilemma must be set in the context of the Civil Procedure Rules 1998 (r 35.10), which also apply to the Commercial Court. These provide that the expert's report must state the substance of all material instructions, whether written or oral, on the basis of which the report was written. The rules also expressly provide that those instructions shall not be privileged against disclosure. However, the court will not order disclosure of any specific document or permit any questioning in court concerning the instructions, other than by the party who instructed the expert, nor will it allow the cross-examination of an expert on his instructions other than in very limited circumstances or when 'it appears to be in the interests of justice'.

These provisions, and the definition of what are 'material instructions', create what is potentially a very difficult and still grey area; but there is no doubt that this approach to the treatment of experts will be incorporated into the family jurisdiction more readily than before and will significantly affect the approach to the instruction of experts generally.

It is, in part, for all these reasons that this book has been co-written by a solicitor and an accountant. No apology is made for the fact that much consideration has been given to how the two professions can work most effectively together to maximise their efforts, avoid duplication and keep costs under control. That is of increasing importance.

The problems which both professions are likely to encounter are varied and challenging: for example, the extent and valuation of holdings in businesses, partnerships and companies; an assessment of the 'real' level of remuneration including perks; any 'historical' property and other asset valuations; unreliable debt and stock figures; market projections and the uncertainty of future earnings; the family involvement; shareholdings retained in UK or offshore trusts (often in children's names); pension funds; how to realise liquid funds and many more.

Amid this, in their search for information, solicitors and accountants are also likely to encounter resistance from a variety of sources: from the other party and, on occasion, from their advisers, business partners, bankers, auditors, shareholders, board members, and/or chief executive. They may be provided with inadequate or out-of-date information requiring them to chase management accounts, draft accounts, annual projections, cash books, bank statements, VAT returns and any other information they can find which will help them to paint an accurate and up-to-date picture. They will need to analyse the payment of salaries, declarations of dividends, use of loan accounts, granting of share options, pension contributions, beneficial loans, expense accounts, company cars, travel allowances, medical cover, and many other perks, to try and establish precisely what the income and benefit level actually is.

In the course of this process, it will be increasingly necessary to identify, as far in advance as is practicable, the likely response of the court to the business picture which is being painted. There will, for example, be few cases where the court will regard favourably the break-up of an established business which is currently providing for the family and is able to continue to do so for the foreseeable future. In such a case, it is therefore inadvisable to produce a detailed report which examines, say, five ways in which the business could be broken up and distributed.

However, the case of *White v White* [2000] 2 FLR 981, HL, in which judgment was given on 31 October 2000, seems likely to have a far-reaching and, at least initially, confusing impact upon ancillary relief law. Many commentators have already expressed their widely varying views on its implications and we deal with the case in some detail in Chapter 1. In broad terms Lord Nicholls, who delivered the leading judgment, highlighted the value of the non-financial contribution to the wealth of the family, arguing that:

'If a husband and wife by their joint efforts over many years, his directly in his business and hers indirectly at home, have built up a valuable business from scratch, why should the claimant wife be confined to the court's assessment of her reasonable requirements, and the husband left with a much larger share?'

In consequence, it seems likely that one major impact of the decision could be in relation to family-run businesses and farming cases; where wives have been genuinely involved in the running of the business, or even if they have made significant efforts in providing for the welfare of the family, then there is likely to be a far greater emphasis on their having an equal share of the value of the business. That may bring with it the need for more precise business valuations, in situations where, in the past, this has been felt unnecessary since there was no prospect of the business being sold. It may also threaten the viability of such family businesses and farming operations if one of the parties is pressing for a sale and a divison of the assets.

The extent of the investigation process, and whether any form of valuation is required, should be evaluated for each individual case. The investigation may reveal a variety of information on income levels – in cash and in kind – as well as past and future earning potential; it may unearth hitherto unknown resources; it may provide information about capital assets, share options, pensions, the scope for raising funds, the plans for a disposal in the short or longer term. It is the role of the professional advisers to consider in each individual case how much of this information is not only relevant and necessary, but also economically justifiable.

Additionally, advisers may have to consider the ability of the husband and wife to continue to work alongside each other in a business, and whether there is a need to look for ways of separating their business interests from their marital relationship while the divorce is being processed. A constructive approach to this particular problem is vital and should also take into consideration the objectives of the client. Are there practical solutions to the problems posed by the case which are likely to be acceptable to both parties (even though fine-tuning may be needed) and which deal with the business position, saving the need for speculative investigation and reporting? Would one party be happy to leave the running of the business to the other, or have they both made significant contributions, are continuing to do so, and will each be reluctant to relinquish involvement? What options will be available to them in that event? Can the business be divided effectively? Are there roles each party can play which will avoid conflict or embarrassment, and how can they be defined? Will new Articles, or a new partnership or shareholders' agreement be needed to deal with the issues that will arise?

There is no doubt that it is increasingly challenging for advisers to find the right balance between resolving all these potential problems and meeting all of their obligations. Advisers must recognise and respond to their clients' instructions and objectives; they must ensure that they do not incur unnecessary costs; they must maintain demanding professional standards and acknowledge and respect their overriding obligation to the court.

The increasing tensions caused by these sometimes conflicting roles are not easily resolved. The expert is most frequently initially recruited as part of the team which investigates and advances one party's contentions and then, as we say above, has to change role to provide the independent professional expert evidence which the court is entitled to expect. The instructing solicitor has to guide the expert through that process (and the dual role) as well as managing many other aspects of the case, and keeping the client informed, involved and reassured.

We hope that this book will help advisers to recognise what steps need to be taken in each case, to take them effectively and economically, to find the balance and draw the line appropriately. Some of the advice is inevitably directed more at solicitors, who generally have the conduct of the case, but forensic accountants practising in the field will also find it of value.

Chapter 1

THE CONDUCT OF THE CASE: SHARING THE RESPONSIBILITIES

INTRODUCTION: THE JUDICIAL APPROACH TO FAMILY BUSINESSES

1.1   There are few more complex problems for a family lawyer or accountant than having to unravel the business affairs of a party to a divorce. Those cases which involve this process are not only complex, but often open to subjective expert valuation and hence to prolonged dispute. The exercise of establishing the true value of the family assets is a critical preliminary to embarking on sensible negotiation or litigation. Where a business is concerned, a wide range of potentially arguable issues may be found.

1.2   In some cases, for example, both spouses may have worked together to build a family business, and both may be equally reluctant to relinquish their role; in other cases, one spouse only may have been involved in the business and the other may know little or nothing about its operation.

1.3   There have been two high profile (and much publicised) cases in the past three years or so, which have offered guidelines to practitioners in cases involving a family business – but there has been a significant contrast in the approach adopted in the two decisions. In the case of *Conran v Conran* [1997] 2 FLR 615, Wilson J embarked upon a detailed analysis of Lady Conran's contribution to the growth of the Conran business empire and concluded that her energy was 'almost as prodigious' as that of her husband. He indicated in his judgment the difficulties he had found in evaluating Lady Conran's efforts:

> 'I find it far from easy to reflect the wife's outstanding contribution in monetary terms. Nor is there even a reported case vaguely analogous to this. All that I can do is to record the detail of the wife's contribution set out in Section D, to apply to it some general considerations; and to trust that I have the instinct and experience to allow justly for it in the ultimate figure.'

1.4   Wilson J made it clear that he found it difficult to blend the assessment of an exceptional contribution with the appraisal of reasonable requirements which had been the guiding factor in such cases for many years. In doing so, he identified the problems in the approach which had been adopted in the Court of Appeal in particular, from the 1970s onwards.

WHITE v WHITE and *N v N*: A FUNDAMENTAL CHANGE OF DIRECTION

1.5 This approach came to a head when Mrs White embarked upon her claim for ancillary relief in Taunton County Court. The case of *White v White* [2000] 2 FLR 981, HL moved from Taunton County Court to the High Court, to the Court of Appeal and eventually to the House of Lords. It had been a long marriage of over 30 years, producing 3 children and a successful dairy farming partnership. The value of the assets was in the region of £4.6 million, and in the High Court, Holman J decided that Mrs White's reasonable requirements were £980,000 (slightly over 20 per cent of the couple's total assets), awarding her a farmhouse home and land, and a *Duxbury* fund of £550,000 to produce a net annual income of £40,000. He rejected Mrs White's request to have enough money to buy her own farm, maintaining that this was not a reasonable requirement, and concluded that it was unwise and unjustified to break up the existing established farming enterprise so that she could embark (much more speculatively, he felt) on another.

1.6 Mrs White appealed to the Court of Appeal and succeeded in increasing the amount of the lump sum payment to £1.5 million. Both parties then appealed to the House of Lords: Mrs White for an increased share of the assets (to not less than 50 per cent, she argued) and Mr White to reinstate the first instance decision. The House of Lords upheld the Court of Appeal's award and Lord Nicholls, who gave the leading judgment, expressed some strong views about the approach which had been adopted by the Court of Appeal until then.

1.7 In an important passage he said:

'But there is one principle of universal application which can be stated with confidence. In seeking to achieve a fair outcome there is no case for discrimination between husband and wife and their respective roles. Typically a husband and wife share the activities of earning money, running their home and caring for their children. Traditionally the husband earned the money and the wife looked after the home and children but this traditional division of labour is no longer the order of the day. Frequently both parents work. Sometimes it is the wife who is the money earner and the husband runs the home and cares for the children during the day. But whatever the division of labour chosen by the husband and wife, or forced upon them by circumstances, fairness requires that this should not prejudice or advantage either party when considering paragraph (f) relating to the parties' contribution ... If in their different spheres each contributed equally to the family then in principle it matters not which of them earned the money and built up the assets. There should be no bias in favour of the money earner and against the home maker and the child carer'.

1.8 He went on to suggest that the judge would always be well advised to check his views on the case 'against the yardstick of equality of division', adding that: 'As a general guide equality should be departed from if and only to the extent that there is good reason for doing so'.

1.9 He resisted the proposal that he should read into the statute a presumption of equal division arguing that this would go beyond the permissible bounds of the interpretation of s 25. However, he reiterated strongly the importance of the non-financial contributions to the welfare of the family and the need for awareness of the extent to which one spouse's business success, achieved by much sustained hard work over many years, may have been made possible or enhanced by the family contribution of the other spouse, a contribution which would require similar effort over a long period.

1.10 He looked again at the approach in the Court of Appeal in *Dart v Dart* [1996] 2 FLR 286 and questioned the leading judgment of Thorpe LJ, preferring the doubts expressed by Peter Gibson and Butler-Sloss LJJ, who in particular felt that the courts might have given too great a weight to reasonable requirements over other criteria, and took the view that if the spouses were in business together, then the traditional reasonable requirements approach was not the most appropriate method to arrive at the post-divorce adjustment of the family finances.

1.11 He found nothing in the statutory provisions or the underlying objective of securing fair financial arrangements to lead him to suppose that the available assets of the respondent became immaterial once the claimant wife's financial needs were satisfied. If the husband and wife had worked together for many years, he in the business and she at home, building up a valuable business from scratch, why should the claimant wife be confined to the court's assessment of her reasonable requirements and the husband left with a much larger share?

1.12 This is perhaps not the place to try to interpret in detail the likely implications of this judgment and a great deal of commentary and speculation have already developed in the period following its publication. Is it applicable only to the 'big money cases'? Will it affect all cases where there is a relatively long marriage and significant contribution from both parties or just 'all cases'? Will it be 're-interpreted' rapidly? What are the reasons to justify 'departing from equality'? Are 'needs' still relevant and if so when, and how? How will fairness be assessed?

1.13 What is clear, is that the court's approach, especially in relation to cases where the husband and wife have been in business together and have, over a period of time, established a successful and substantial enterprise, is likely to be significantly affected by the House of Lords' decision in *White*, and that in such cases it will be far harder to justify a departure from the yardstick of equality.

1.14 If that is right, then it follows that whilst every effort should be made to avoid too intensive and expensive investigation procedures, more detailed business valuations may now be needed and a more rigorous approach to the options for realisation of the business assets may be required. A 'fully entitled' wife, if it is indeed she, will be far less inclined to allow the family business to continue to flourish in the husband's exclusive ownership, accepting a capital settlement sufficient merely to meet her 'reasonable requirements'. If equality does become the yardstick in these cases, then, subject to the practicalities of overcoming illiquidity, the *White* decision could pose a serious threat to the viability of family businesses upon divorce.

1.15 Practitioners will now more frequently have to take careful and detailed instructions on the financial history, and on contribution – in all its guises – both in relation to the home and the business and financial picture. The Form E sections dealing with these issues (and possibly those dealing with conduct too) will be more comprehensive, and inevitably more contentious. Proportionality must, however, remain a key concern.

1.16 There will also be cases where there has been only a modest contribution, where the ownership of the business is entirely in the hands of one spouse and where it is entirely dependent on the skills, drive, acumen, and management of that person. Alternatively, although not directly involved in running the business, a spouse may be a minority or majority shareholder and here the interests of other shareholders or partners will have to be considered carefully. In each such case, 'fairness' and the extent of any departure from the 'yardstick of equality' will still need very careful judgment.

1.17 Another possible consequence of the *White* decision will be a move to increased forum shopping, away from this jurisdiction, in those cases where to one client at least the concept of an equal division is unattractive. Commentators have also suggested that there may be an increase in the use of pre-nuptial agreements, to exclude the prospect of an equal division where the parties are prepared to contract out. Although this may come to pass, the reality is that at the present time pre-nuptial agreements are not binding under English law, only, at the most, a factor which the court would take into consideration at some level. The investment of too much time, cost, investigation, negotiation and potential confrontation prior to marriage in drafting such agreements will always have to be set against the uncertainty of their ultimate effect and relevance. When a family business may be regulated by a shareholder or partnership agreement, and/or the Memorandum and Articles of the company, and where service contracts and other employment arrangements may also be in place, it may in any event be untenable to place yet a further layer of control on top of that in the form of a pre-nuptial agreement.

1.18 Very often the income which is generated by the business will continue to be crucial, following the divorce, in maintaining the family home, the children's education, and the lifestyle of the parties. The threat to the stability of the family if the business fails or suffers badly as a consequence of misguided confrontation, is a very genuine one. A recent survey has highlighted the difficulties which already exist in maintaining a family business through the generations; it seems that few make it to the second generation, and fewer still survive to the third or fourth generation. The increase in the rate of divorce (and the *White* approach) poses yet another threat.

1.19 The most recent case-law on the question of liquidity and the scope to raise funds stems from a case decided in Liverpool before Coleridge J and reported as *N v N (Financial Provision: Sale of Company)* [2001] 2 FLR 69. In one sense the case is a salutary one in its approach to the possible dismantling of a long-established family company, but in another it is the logical and realistic extension of the principles established in the *White* case and it addresses head on the issue of balancing fairness with illiquidity of assets.

1.20 In *N v N*, the court was dealing with a marriage of 14 years and there were three children aged 13, 11 and 4. The husband had an interest in a number of professional partnerships and was also a business entrepreneur with an interest in two companies which was ultimately valued at around £2 milllion gross, or £1.75 million net of capital gains tax.

1.21 There were other assets including the former home, commercial properties, a pension fund and loan accounts, but there were acute liquidity problems and the only immediately available family funds were around £200,000.

1.22 The husband argued that the wife should receive very significantly less than an equal share, and that the court should be constrained by the illiquidity of the family assets, and also by the fact that the wife was relatively young, the marriage was not of long duration and his contributions were far greater than hers, and that there was a substantial increase in the values in the period since the separation.

1.23 Coleridge J appeared to hear some of these arguments sympathetically, to the extent that he awarded the wife a lump sum of £1 million, approximately 39 per cent of the assets, to be effected by a transfer of the former house and three lump sum payment instalments, culminating in a final payment of £650,000 some three years after the hearing, protected by full security pending payment, and almost certainly involving the sale or restructuring of the husband's company shareholdings.

1.24 Whilst acknowledging that the decision in *White* would require a new approach and would result in many cases in higher awards for wives, he went on to say:

> 'As is glaringly apparent from this case, the theory behind *White* is one thing. But the actual practicalities involved in valuing, dividing up, and/or realising certain species of assets make the attaining of the *White* objective sometimes either impossible or only achievable at a cost which may not overall be in the family's best interests. In this regard of one thing I am convinced. I am sure the House of Lords did not intend courts to exercise their far-reaching powers to achieve equality on paper if in doing so they, Samson-like, brought down or crippled the whole family's financial edifice to the ultimate detriment of the children (whose interests, of course, remain the top priority in this and every case). More than ever in the new climate, especially where the facts are similar to the present (where the award is likely to be larger than before *White*), the court, in my judgment, must be creative and sensitive to achieve an orderly redistribution of wealth.'

1.25 Later in his judgment he tackled the difficult issue of the increase in the turnover of the business from 1997, when the parties separated, to 2001, the date of the hearing, and the impact of this upon the values of the companies. Counsel for the wife had argued that, traditionally, applications for financial provision have always been approached on the basis of the values at the date when the hearing takes place. Although the judge acknowledged that in most cases that would be the appropriate date, he took the view that the court:

'must have an eye to the valuation at the date of separation where there has been a very significant change accounted for by more than just inflation or deflation.'

He went on to say:

'In this case the increase in value is attributable to extra investment of time, effort and money by the husband since separation and I do take into account the exceptionally steep increase in the turnover figures since the date of the separation. However, having done so it must be put in the context of the wife's continuing contribution too which similarly did not cease at the date of separation. She too has continued to play the valuable part that she had done throughout the marriage, in looking after the home and the children.'

1.26 Balancing a number of other factors which he deals with in the judgment, he reached the conclusion that the right figure for the wife was to be the lump sum of £1 million, acknowledging that it reflected her entitlement in accordance with the latest principles, and that it more than met her reasonable needs, although adding 'that is no longer any kind of ceiling in a case of this value'.

1.27 He emphasised that the husband had to be given every opportunity to raise the funds to buy out the wife's liquidated share over a reasonable period of time and set a timetable which in effect gave the husband three years to raise the necessary funds, the vast bulk of which would only be payable at the end of the third year.

1.28 He commented that the liquidation of the group, or the husband's shareholding in it, was an inevitable consequence of the break up of the marriage, and he added one final paragraph at the end of his judgment which bears repeating:

'However, I think it must now be taken that those old taboos against selling the goose that lays the golden egg have largely been laid to rest; some would say not before time. Nowadays the goose may well have to go to market for sale, but if it is necessary to sell her it is essential that her condition be such that her egg laying abilities are damaged as little as possible in the process. Otherwise there is a danger that the full value of the goose will not be achieved and the underlying basis of any order will turn out to be flawed.'

1.29 There is no doubt that this judgment (which it is thought may yet go to appeal) addresses one of the key issues raised by *White* and confronts it firmly, realistically and constructively. The defence of illiquidity can clearly no longer be guaranteed to succeed in resisting a properly formulated claim, and although the ultimate outcome will depend in many cases on the age of children, on their future needs, on the ability of the parties to support them if the family business is dismantled, it is apparent from this decision that in future the court will not hesitate to conclude that, in the absence of liquidity, fairness may demand 'the sale of the goose'.

1.30   An accurate analysis of the business interests of the parties may involve a wide range of issues: a valuation of the shareholding itself, and of the underlying company assets such as properties, cars, stock and goodwill; an analysis of the true earnings of the shareholders or partners, including salary, dividends, benefits in kind, both disclosed and non-disclosed; an examination of the scope for raising funds to facilitate a settlement; and an understanding of the tax consequences of extracting funds or imposing changes on the business structure.

1.31   Even in the more straightforward cases, great care is needed to ensure that the facts and figures are properly understood and (if it proves necessary), presented clearly to the court. At the same time, the expense of what can often be, unavoidably, a complex and specialist exercise must be balanced against the court's strictures on incurring unnecessary costs.

GUIDELINES AND GROUND RULES

1.32   In theory, the guidelines are simple enough. As Anthony Lincoln J held in *P v P (Financial Provision)* [1989] 2 FLR 241, a case dealing in part with business valuations, the proper approach is to take a broad and general consideration of the resources of the parties, and against that, to assess the wife's reasonable requirements and the husband's ability to meet those requirements. In that case, Lincoln J concluded that all that was required was the broadest evaluation of the company's worth in order to assist the court to decide the wife's reasonable requirements. If there was liquidity in the company which could be realised to meet her requirements, then the final order would take that liquidity into account. If there was none, in the sense that the company (the source of the breadwinner's income) would be damaged, then the court should look elsewhere.

1.33   However, it is never quite that simple. In his opening words in *P v P*, the judge said:

> 'Once again I am confronted with the fact that the total realizable funds of the family have been severely reduced by the incurring of vast costs by both sides in order to resolve an issue as to the value of their respective shareholding. In the outcome that issue proved to be of little or no importance. In my view legal advisers in cases such as this should strain to adopt any viable alternative, compatible with the interests of their clients, in order to avoid costly valuations

detrimental to both parties and particularly to the children. I do not believe that Parliament when enacting s 25 of the Matrimonial Causes Act 1973 envisaged such detailed, prolonged and damaging investigations.'

As Lincoln J said, *P v P* was a case where: 'The accountants for each side have reached vastly divergent conclusions, as they so often do'. The difference in that case was £1.6 million.

1.34   Any practitioner who has not read the entire report on *P v P* would be well advised to do so, together with a number of the other major cases in this field, many of which will be referred to in this book. The seminal case was *Evans v Evans* [1990] 1 FLR 319 in which Booth J, with the concurrence of the President of the Family Division, commenced her judgment with some general guidelines to be followed by the practitioner in the preparation of a substantial ancillary relief case.

1.35   The key points were:

- confine affidavit evidence to the facts and keep affidavits to a minimum on each side;
- use one comprehensive questionnaire each whenever possible;
- agree joint valuations and reports wherever possible;
- do not undertake an expensive and meaningless exercise to achieve a precise valuation of a private company;
- ensure professional witnesses avoid a partisan approach and maintain proper professional standards;
- keep clients informed as to costs and bear in mind the desirability of achieving a settlement throughout the proceedings.

1.36   Most practitioners will now (or certainly should) be familiar with the new Family Proceedings Rules (see para **1.43** below) which reflect much of the basic wisdom of the *Evans* judgment, refined through the Ancillary Relief Pilot Scheme, into their current final form. The temptation which practitioners often faced to continue with investigations, under pressure from clients who were determined to unearth what they believed to be their spouse's buried treasure, is now subject to the often strict control of the court on the First Appointment. Those excessively lengthy questionnaires, often taken unedited straight from the word processor; the lengthy exchanges of correspondence; over-zealous accounting investigations; and partisan valuations will all significantly reduce under the watchful and rigorous eyes of experienced district judges who are united in their attempt to reduce the extent and expense of bitterly contested and expensive litigation. The procedure requires very thorough disclosure at the outset and thereafter controlled questions linked to the issues in the case; it will ensure a more disciplined approach, but practitioners must still always ensure that they are not dissuaded from a proper and thorough investigation when it is clearly necessary.

1.37   Experience to date suggests that when these matters are handled properly, the court continues to understand and accept the need for a thorough enquiry. It will be appreciative and welcoming of the assistance of expert evidence from professionals who are able to prepare thorough and helpful reports, who can negotiate with their opposite number constructively and effectively, and who will often produce agreement on a number of issues, and narrow the areas of disagreement elsewhere. The issues raised below in Chapter 8 on 'The Husband's Hidden Wealth' demonstrate clearly the challenges which the practitioner will meet in the more complex and difficult cases. There is still, however, a great deal to be done and it is hoped that this book will play a part in the further education process.

1.38   The following sets out some of the basic ground rules (this is addressed primarily, although not exclusively, to solicitors):

– understand the new Rules and procedures and practice directions;
– if proceedings are not yet issued, understand the pre-action protocol and note the guidance there on the use of experts;
– look carefully at the overall value of the case, the information available to date, the broad likely outcome (if this can be predicted) and think hard and rigorously about what further information is justifiably needed, and how best to obtain it; draft your statement of issues carefully with this in mind;
– consider whether expert assistance is needed and, if so, at what stage – timing is important;
– select experts carefully; discuss the decisions with the client and with counsel, if appropriate;
– ensure that everyone involved – solicitor, counsel, experts, and client – works as a team (never forget that the client is a vital member of this team);
– ensure everyone is aware of the timetable as it evolves;
– plan a clear (but perhaps flexible) strategy; from the first meetings, to the drafting of the Form E, statement of issues and questionnaires, through the negotiation and preparation of reports, and, on each of the hearings;
– monitor costs throughout, including the experts, and keep the client fully informed.

SPIRALLING COSTS – THE CRITICISMS

1.39   The guidelines in *Evans v Evans* have, or should have, served as a blueprint for the professions working in ancillary relief applications ever since November 1989. Regrettably, however, it is inescapably true that the criticisms on costs have continued both from the Family Division judges and from district judges across the country, as well as from within the professions, not least in some lively correspondence between practitioners. The new procedures have not, and will not, eliminate those criticisms. It is also notable that many courts outside London find the costs of central London firms disproportionately high – and say so.

1.40   Criticism on costs has continued at judicial level and the observations of Thorpe J in *F v F (Ancillary Relief: Substantial Assets)* [1995] 2 FLR 45 concerning the costs in the preparation of the case were trenchant. He took the view that the expenditure on costs at that level was unacceptable and he highlighted in particular the excessive involvement of professional witnesses who had been instructed unilaterally and encouraged to put their case as high as possible; the lack of opportunity given to the experts to meet and discuss matters in advance of the trial and the need for them to strive for objectivity and the middle ground. His judgment has encouraged judicial intervention in the involvement of experts and the new Rules have also ensured that their roles are carefully monitored.

1.41   Thorpe J also added a number of comments on the scale of the correspondence and the need to adopt a non-adversarial approach to the preparation of the case, and he referred back to the *Evans* guidelines on a number of occasions. He identified the fact that powerful and influential clients may be inclined and, indeed, able to dictate to their advisers the way in which they wish to conduct the case and he emphasised the need to stand against that in spite of the pressures it may create. There is a need for all advisers in family work to maintain a professional independence and integrity, however difficult and (in the client's perception) unsatisfactory that may be.

1.42   In the high profile case of *Dart v Dart* [1996] 2 FLR 286, Thorpe LJ commented as follows in his judgment:

> 'In addition to the costs incurred by the wife in challenging jurisdiction in London she has incurred costs in Michigan stated to amount to £1m. Her solicitor's own client costs in the London ancillary relief proceedings are stated to total £877,025. Of her total solicitor's own client bill in London put at £1.4m only £30,000 has been paid on account, the rest of the work being done on credit. The husband's ancillary relief costs amount to £477,127. Johnson J in his judgment described the preparation of the case in these terms:
>
>> "The extravagance of the preparations in this case defies moderate description. The husband's initial disclosure was in my view adequate, I would say more than adequate, for the purpose of these English proceedings. None the less on the wife's behalf repeated requests were made for yet further information and yet further documents. The result is that there have been in court an astonishing 72 ringbinders all of substantial size. The wife's repeated questions and demands for information were aimed at challenging the husband's present wealth and the various routes by which it came to him; and the past expenditure of the family. The information and documents which were provided by the husband were provided voluntarily and the court was never asked to adjudicate on the justification for the wife's demands. No doubt the husband was advised that to make an issue about the matter would create delay and perhaps even more expense; and that in any event the information might have to be forthcoming in proceedings in the USA.
>>
>> Be that as it may the consequence has been that the wife's legal costs in the various English proceedings have been a staggering £1,366,400 of which

£877,025 is attributable to her costs in this application. The husband's total costs are £801,699 of which £477,127 is attributable to this application.

The responsibility for this extravagant, and indeed scandalous, waste of money does not, I suspect, lie with the wife's English lawyers but rather with her attorneys in the USA. I note from the bundle of correspondence that when an open offer of settlement was made on behalf of the husband, the wife's solicitors made no effective response but asked only that any proposal for settlement should be directed by the husband's English solicitors to the wife's attorneys in Michigan."

I agree with every word of the quoted passage save that I have to wonder whether the exoneration of the wife's English lawyers is not overcharitable. Whilst it is of course impossible to allocate responsibility for such scandalous expenditure there is at least a presumption of responsibility in the wife's English lawyers that would not be easily rebutted. Costs of this magnitude are almost unknown in this jurisdiction. They are a condemnation of our present procedures. On 1 October 1996 new procedures are to be put on trial. These new procedures are designed to ensure among other objectives that the court and not the parties controls the escalation of costs.'

THE FAMILY PROCEEDINGS (AMENDMENT NO 2) RULES 1999 ('THE NEW RULES')

1.43 The new Family Proceedings Rules came into effect on 5 June 2000 and apply to all proceedings commenced on or after that date. Where proceedings have been commenced before 5 June 2000, the court has a discretion to direct that the provisions of the new rules shall apply. These rules are the culmination of several years' negotiation and discussion between the senior judiciary, the Family Law Bar Association, the Solicitors Family Law Association, the Lord Chancellor's Department, several district judges from outside London and a number of other interested and influential parties, and they follow the successful introduction of the Ancillary Relief Pilot Scheme in a cross-section of courts throughout the country.

1.44 It is beyond the scope of this book to deal in detail with the new rules, about which entire textbooks have already been written. However, they undoubtedly represent a dramatic change for many practitioners, in particular those who have not had experience of the pilot scheme, and they are certainly designed to answer many of the criticisms and concerns which have been expressed by the judiciary over recent years, if only because it will be they who, to a large degree, will now control the running of the cases.

The overriding objective of the new rules is to enable the court to deal with cases justly, as defined in r 2.51B. There is an emphasis on the active management of cases, which includes encouraging co-operation in the conduct of the proceedings; encouraging the parties to settle through mediation where appropriate; identifying the issues at an early stage; regulating the extent of disclosure and expert evidence so that they are proportionate to the issues in question; fixing timetables; controlling the progress of the case; and ensuring that the trial proceeds quickly and efficiently.

1.45 The overriding Woolf principle of proportionality features heavily. Cases should be dealt with in ways which are proportionate to the amounts involved, the importance and the complexity of the case, and the financial position of each party. Costs are under scrutiny and pressure as never before.

1.46 It is too early to see precisely what the impact of this new overriding approach will be. Experience already suggests that the new procedure, in providing for early and strictly timetabled disclosure; a rigorously controlled First Appointment, where further disclosure is permitted only to the extent that it is strictly related to the issues in the case; and for the control of expert evidence, is curtailing excessive and unjustifiable disclosure. The introduction of a financial dispute resolution appointment, requiring offers to be made by each side in advance and encouraging every effort to settle, all underpinned by the extremely strict (and arguably excessively punitive) costs provisions, is having its effect.

1.47 The provisions in relation to use of expert evidence are dealt with below (see para **1.51**) and must be read and understood; the guidance in this book must be read in conjunction with those rules where applicable.

DECIDING WHEN AND HOW TO INSTRUCT AN ACCOUNTANT

1.48 The solicitor will know that many applications for ancillary relief will not require the expert assistance of an accountant, and even some of the more high-value and difficult cases can be handled without their help. In each case, the solicitor, counsel and client should give careful consideration to the question of whether or not such assistance is required, and at what stage it will best assist in helping them to prepare and present their client's claims more effectively. They must also assess whether the costs of such a course can be justified and, if so, how controls and constraints can be placed upon the investigation to be carried out by the solicitor and accountant, to keep matters under review and avoid the risk of criticism.

1.49 In the past, and certainly until the introduction of the Finance Act 1988, the advice of an accountant was often sought in connection with the issues surrounding maintenance. Payers of maintenance were entitled to claim tax relief on monies paid to a spouse and children under a court order, or pursuant to an agreement. Tax relief was also available on payments made to a child or children even in circumstances where that child or those children were living with the payer. *Sherdley v Sherdley* [1988] AC 213 concerned the issue of school fee agreements and confronted the House of Lords with some complex areas of tax law which, in the opinion of some, they did not address entirely satisfactorily. In those (now perhaps distant) times, the advice of an accountant was often essential in calculating the most tax-effective way of paying and receiving maintenance, and such assistance was often called on in advance of any court hearing, or in the course of settlement negotiations, to avoid irretrievable errors being made. The accountant would also often play a subsequent role in monitoring tax returns, claiming relief, and dealing with any problems which arose.

1.50 The Finance Act 1988 greatly simplified the tax implications of maintenance orders and agreements, by abolishing the entitlement to relief and thereby enabling the slow removal of most of the complexities which had arisen in this area. All remaining relief has, in any event, now been entirely phased out. There are, however, many other very important areas where an accountant's guidance can be vital in assisting solicitors, either in the preparation and presentation of their clients' claims for financial provision, or equally, in resisting claims made against their clients.

New Rules governing the use of expert evidence

1.51 Following the Woolf Report and the introduction of the Civil Procedure Rules 1998 (CPR 1998), it seems likely that the provisions of those rules governing expert evidence would be incorporated within the Family Proceedings Rules 1991 (FPR 1991) in their entirety. For various reasons that did not happen, but r 2.61C of the FPR 1991 (as inserted by the Family Proceedings (Amendment No 2) Rules 1999 (the new Rules)) provides that the CPR 1998, rr 35.1–35.14 relating to expert evidence, with appropriate modifications and with one or two exceptions, 'apply to all ancillary relief proceedings'. In summary, those rules provide as follows.

1. There is a duty to restrict expert evidence to that evidence which is reasonably required to resolve proceedings; again, the issue of proportionality arises here.
2. Experts have an overriding duty to the court, and that duty overrides any obligation to the party instructing them or to the person who may pay them.
3. Expert evidence must be in the form of a written report, but neither party may call an expert or put in a report without the leave of the court. It is necessary to identify the field in which the expert evidence is required, and where possible to identify the appropriate expert. The leave of the court will be given rigorously and the court has power to limit the amount of fees which may be recoverable from the other party.
4. The party who has not instructed the expert witness may on one occasion put written questions to the expert upon the report, for the purpose of clarification, and the answers to those questions will be treated as part of the report; the failure to answer any such questions may result in the evidence being disallowed or prevent recovery of costs.

5.   Where both parties wish to submit expert evidence on a particular issue the court may direct that evidence should be given by one expert only and may direct the manner in which that expert is to be selected if that cannot be agreed; directions may also be given on the steps to be taken by the expert, the requirement for information to be made available to the expert, and the arrangements for payment.

6.   The report produced by the expert must comply with the specific standards set out in the CPR 1998, r 35.10. Any party may use a disclosed expert's report as evidence, conversely if the report is not disclosed, then it may not be relied upon without the court's consent. CPR 1998, r 35.10 provides that the expert's report must state the substance of all material instructions, whether written or oral, on the basis of which the report was written, and that those instructions should not be privileged against disclosure. As we have explained, the court will not, in relation to those instructions, order disclosure of any specific document or permit any questioning in court other than by the party who instructed the expert, unless it is satisfied that there are reasonable grounds to consider the statement of instructions to be inaccurate or incomplete. Cross-examination of the expert on his instructions will be permitted only when 'it appears to be in the interests of justice'.

Guidance is urgently needed on what constitutes 'material instructions' for the purposes of this rule, since without it unintentional breaches of requirements by experts and instructing solicitors are likely to arise, causing consequent disputes and additional cost.

Note also that the pre-application protocol contains very specific guidance about the use of expert evidence and failure to follow it could again result in a costs penalty, further down the line. (See *Practice Direction (Ancillary Relief Procedure 2000)* (25 May 2000) [2000] 1 FLR 997.)

7.   The court may at any stage direct a discussion between experts for the purpose of requiring them to identify issues between them and, where possible, reach agreement on those issues; this is an approach already adopted frequently within the Family Division.

8.   The expert may ask the court for directions as to how to carry out his function without giving notice to any party.

1.52   Previous experience under the pilot scheme regime suggested judges would be hesitant about ordering expert evidence on the First Appointment if basic information could be provided, or alternatively, they might order a restricted report to keep costs at a proportionate level, on the basis that if matters were not resolved at the FDR then a fresh view would have to be taken of the necessity for more detailed (and expensive) evidence.

1.53   It is already the case that district judges are pressing for evidence on such matters as property valuations to be prepared by a single appointed expert, and there is very considerable and unresolved debate at present about the role of the single, jointly appointed, expert accountant in matrimonial proceedings.

Recognising the need to instruct an accountant – a checklist

1.54 Practitioners will always have to determine in each case whether it is one which warrants the expense of accountancy or other financial advice and, if so, when it should be sought. The following questions may help to determine the issue.

- Does the client need to present their statement of assets and liabilities in Form E in such complex terms that the input of either an existing accountant or a specially appointed accountant is necessary, either for presentation and clarity, or for analysis at this early stage – or even simply for approval?

- Is assistance needed in analysing, evaluating or challenging the information supplied by the other party, whether it be business or company accounts, complex income documentation, several years of copy bank statements, or other complex financial information? Is a search for hidden assets necessary?

- Is advice needed specifically on the valuation of interests in businesses, partnerships or private companies, either to produce 'the broadest evaluation of the company's worth', or where it may be proposed that there should be a sale or transfer of such interests between the parties or otherwise?

- Do the tax implications of a proposed settlement need consideration?

- Is it necessary to calculate the size and appropriate capital sum to be paid to a spouse on a clean break, under the guidelines set out in *Duxbury v Duxbury* [1987] 1 FLR 7 (ie where the fiscal and financial position of the recipient spouse needs careful consideration and where the constraints and limitations of the *Duxbury* approach have to be taken into particular account)?

- Is it necessary to advise on the implications of capital gains tax in cases where an asset has to be sold to produce funds or where it is proposed to transfer property between spouses?

- Is advice needed on the fiscal implications of one party being resident overseas for tax purposes or holding trusts overseas, and/or where it may be intended to remit overseas funds into the jurisdiction to provide regular income, or when capital has to be raised in a tax-efficient manner?

- Is it necessary to assess the impact of settlement proposals in relation to their fiscal implications, their investment prospects, and their acceptability generally to the client; or to assist in assessing what a party's budgetary needs really are?

- Have negotiations progressed to a point where there is a need for consultation between accountants to resolve as many issues as possible between them prior to the hearing, either pursuant to a directions order or in anticipation of one; and where ultimately accountants' reports are likely to be required?

– Generally, is there a significant dispute between the parties as to key financial matters in which an independent assessment is required?

– Is this a case where the evidence of an expert witness, adopting an unbiased approach, is likely to be viewed by the court as more detached and genuinely independent than a solicitor or counsel presenting his or his client's assessment of a business asset? Bear in mind that it is almost inevitable that a professional report on a complex financial issue will carry more weight than even the most thoroughly researched submissions of solicitor and counsel.

– Is this a case where there may be scope for a single, jointly appointed expert to deal with specific issues?

The above checklist is not exhaustive; there will be other situations in which a careful and rigorous analysis of the issues will indicate the need for expert financial advice.

1.55 Some extremely helpful and straightforward guidance is provided by the regularly updated *Directory of Expert Witnesses* (Law Society), which provides a Code of Practice for expert witnesses engaged by solicitors, Guidelines for Solicitors instructing expert witnesses, advice on the role of the expert in litigation and on choosing the right expert, and a specific section on family law cases, including financial proceedings and the use of forensic accountants. For those not experienced in the use of expert witnesses, the *Directory* is helpful and accessible; even for those who are, a review of these sections would be useful.

Fee arrangements

1.56 Confusion may sometimes arise (and not just on fees) because the responsibility for instructing the accountant may be shared informally between solicitor and client. It is essential to be clear who is to be responsible for all the fees and disbursements to be incurred. The solicitor may accept that his firm will pay, and undertake to do so with whatever qualifications may be appropriate. In such a case, the arrangement should be clarified in an exchange of letters. Alternatively, the client may prefer to pay the accountant directly. Care should be taken with this approach, as it may reduce the image of professional independence which it is important to preserve.

Extent and expense of the accountant's involvement

1.57 The solicitor must bear in mind the new Rules and consider carefully the extent to which the work is necessary; its range and probable cost; the role of the accountant as the case progresses in reporting, negotiating and giving evidence. The initial application for directions concerning expert evidence would usually be made at the First Appointment and will not be granted without good reason. A full detailed (and expensive) report may be inappropriate (or disproportionate) prior to the FDR and many district judges wil' consider delaying full reports and enquiries until after the FDR, and only then if it is clearly necessary. The observation of Booth J in *Evans v Evans* remains as valid as ever (save only for the impact of *White*):

> 'While it may be necessary to obtain a broad assessment of the value of a shareholding in a private company, it is inappropriate to undertake an expensive and meaningless exercise to achieve a precise valuation of a private company which will not be sold.'

Drafting the Form E

1.58   Generally, the Form E will be prepared by the solicitor and client together, perhaps with assistance from counsel. It must reflect accurately and comprehensively the financial information which is being disclosed with it or which will be disclosed later, and if there are complexities and ambiguities, then an accountant's early participation in drafting may be essential. It is extremely unhelpful and damaging to serve a sworn Form E by the client which is then contradicted or undermined by documentary evidence disclosed later, and which was available at the time it was originally drafted.

Full, frank and clear disclosure

1.59   The preparation of a client's financial disclosure is a vital stage in the proceedings, whether in the Form E, in disclosed documents, or in answers to a questionnaire. The disclosure must be full, frank and clear. If the solicitor is facing difficulty in obtaining all necessary information from the client perhaps because of its complexity, or through a lack of co-operation from the client or the auditors, then the assistance of an accountant at that stage can be supportive and valuable.

Analysing the other party's disclosure: using other experts

1.60   When the Form E and disclosed documentation of the other party is available for consideration, it may be of such complexity, or sheer volume, that an accountancy investigation and a clear analysis is necessary. It may also be at this point that further expert evidence is required.

1.61   For example, the disclosure of complex or confusing pension details may require the assistance of an actuary or specialist pensions consultant; discouraging projections as to the future prospects of the business may suggest the need for expert evidence from that particular industry sector; where property issues arise (whether in relation to matrimonial property or business property reflected in the accounts at historic values), specialist valuation advice may be required. If concerns of this kind arise, the team of advisers should consider with the client what further specialist advice is needed, and determine such issues as whether a written report will suffice, or if oral evidence is likely to be required; whether the evidence can be agreed in advance; and whether the directions given provide for such further evidence, or leave will be required.

Where possible, anticipate the directions which may be needed on the First Appointment. Failing that, if the FDR is not successful, then the advisers should ensure they are ready to deal with the issue of further directions at its conclusion, and have given the matter sufficient thought. In the context of an FDR after a long and ultimately fruitless negotiation and perhaps amid disappointment and frustration, it is easy to overlook key points in the preparation for the contested hearing.

Drafting the questionnaire

1.62   Having reviewed the other party's disclosure and Form E, the solicitor may then wish to question the other side upon it. So far as possible, those questions should be contained in one comprehensive questionnaire and should not be made on a piecemeal basis at different times. This guideline is rarely followed; often it is impossible to do so. In practice, the answers to a first set of questions often provoke consequential questions. As cases develop, new issues may emerge, requiring different questions to be asked. The financial circumstances of the parties may change as the case progresses over a period of months; again such changes may demand fresh investigation. However, the new Rules require the questionnaires to be exchanged well in advance of the First Appointment, and in effect, cross-referenced with the statement of issues, so care and rigour are essential from the outset. The opportunity to ask further questions may be restricted.

1.63   The aim should therefore be to draft one comprehensive questionnaire and it can be very helpful to involve the accountant (if he has not previously been instructed) in preparing it. This will help to ensure that all the issues the accountant may wish to raise, and the documents he may wish to see, can be referred to at that stage. It also avoids the danger of serving the questionnaire without such input, and only realising after obtaining the initial information that the accountant in fact needed the answers to many further questions, and to see many additional documents. The court will deal severely with excessive or repetitive questionnaires; it is increasingly essential to get the process right from the outset.

1.64   Be careful also in relation to the much stricter timetables now imposed by the new Rules. Forms E must be exchanged five weeks prior to the first appointment, and questionnaires and statements of issues 14 days before. Thus if the other side's Form E is a week late (by no means unusual), then the time available to consider that Form E and its annexed documents, and to decide what questions can properly be raised and what further documents requested, and to link that with the concise statement of issues, is very tight indeed. The new accountants will not find it easy to meet these deadlines and it is essential to ensure that they are well briefed in advance, on standby to respond rapidly when the information is received, and able to deliver within the timetable. Again, given the reluctance of the court to allow very many bites at the cherry, it is essential that all the questions are in place in the first questionnaire, if at all possible.

MANAGING THE DOCUMENTATION – A CHECKLIST

1.65   The management of documentation in ancillary relief applications is an art in itself. There are a number of basic and sensible steps which can mitigate the problems that arise, and help ease the burden on any expert you may instruct, by ensuring that the information supplied to him is ordered and coherent. The following basic steps should be borne in mind:

–   keep the documents provided by the client separate from those provided by the other side;

–   keep a clearly marked set of Forms E, exhibits, chronologies, statements of issues, costs estimates, questionnaires and answers to questionnaires for each party;

–   as documents arrive, file them properly in ring binders, in sequence and clearly indexed; do not paginate prematurely, as the numbering may change;

–   ensure that all the team are working from the same set of documents and that each of them has a set in sequence and clearly indexed; this will ensure that any cross-references and discussions at conferences, meetings and interlocutory hearings can be effective and no time is wasted;

–   build up proposed trial bundles piece by piece as the case develops, and begin the process of agreeing bundles between solicitors, counsel and experts in good time prior to the hearing;

–   agreeing bundles, pagination and indexation are painstaking but vital, so do not leave it all until the last moment; sensible co-operation between solicitors, counsel and experts is invaluable in this procedure;

–   be aware that financial information will usually have to be updated as a case progresses, especially given the length of the time between fixing the trial date and the full hearing (often six months or more). Whichever party is the client, consider the need to update company information, bank statements, credit card statements, the outgoings budget, pension and property valuations and any other key financial information.

1.66   In the context of requirements for bundling, and preparation of bundles for the court, the *Practice Direction (Family Proceedings: Court Bundles)* (10 March 2000) [2000] 1 FLR 536 issued by the President concerning court bundles is fundamental reading, and is already being very strictly enforced, with punitive costs orders having already been made against defaulting solicitors. Any practitioner doubting the importance of this practice direction should read the judgment of Wall J in *Re CH (A Minor)* [2000] 2 FCR 193 in which, relying on CPR 1998, r 44.14, he disallowed fees (by 50 per cent) on the basis that in his view the case took 'approximately four times as long as it should have done' in court.

1.67 If an accountant or other expert is to be instructed, counsel will wish to arrange a meeting at a relatively early stage in order to discuss the parameters of the expert's brief. At later stages, meetings should be arranged to discuss draft reports, to review the opposition's submissions, and consider the strategy for the hearing. The introduction of the expert to counsel should not be left to the last moment.

INSTRUCTION OF AN ACCOUNTANT BY THE OTHER PARTY

1.68 Even if the appointment of an accountant is a reactive or defensive decision, it may still be a wise one. For example, one party may instruct accountants, indicate this to the other side and apply to the court for leave to produce their expert's report, and for appropriate directions as to meetings, agreement of reports where possible etc, in a case where the other party may not have intended to instruct an expert at all. This may occur, for example, when the onus is upon a wife's advisers to analyse a husband's business or company and general financial position, and they decide that they need expert assistance in doing so; whereas the husband and his advisers may have until then assumed or believed that they could deal with all the issues which would arise without the need for additional help.

1.69 When such a situation arises, the party who had not initially intended to seek accountancy advice must give careful consideration to doing so. There may be cost constraints, and a natural reluctance to incur unnecessary expense or increase the size of the team; there may be resistance from the client for other reasons. There will also be a need to obtain the appropriate direction from the court. However, the client could be faced with a significant disadvantage if careful and thorough forensic accountancy advice and guidance is available to the other party alone. In addition, in the context of meetings between experts to consider whether agreement can be reached, or for preparing reports and/or narrowing the outstanding issues, it will be far harder for the solicitor confronted with a specialist accountant to act effectively on his own without specialist help, while conducting all the other aspects of the case.

Chapter 2

SELECTING AND BRIEFING THE ACCOUNTANT

INTRODUCTION

2.1   In the previous chapter, we considered the timing of the appointment of an accountant and other experts, and the reasons for doing so. This chapter will deal with the equally, indeed crucially, important issues of the selection and briefing of the expert. Many of the points made in this chapter are addressed principally to solicitors. All must be considered in the light of the court's approach as explained in the previous chapter. The very clear move towards increased appointments of single joint experts in matrimonial cases will not necessarily exclude accountants, however much their dual role, as explained above, causes complications. Careful guidance and control will be essential from the initial instructions (possibly open to court scrutiny) through to the preparation of a report to the court. It is now vital that solicitors and accountants are fully conversant with the rules governing the appointment of experts.

SELECTING THE AUDITOR OR AN INDEPENDENT ACCOUNTANT

2.2   Once the decision has been made to obtain expert accountancy advice the next question will be whom to appoint. Where acting for the owner and shareholder of a business, when the value of that business will form a vital part of the client's assets, the immediate question will be whether to instruct as experts the client's current company auditors. The apparent advantages of doing so may be their experience and loyalty to the business which can lead to an almost irresistible temptation to appoint the current auditors or other close and regular financial advisers to act on the client's behalf in the matrimonial litigation.

2.3   Among the considerations in selecting experts can also be the thought that the current auditors may be a less expensive choice because of their intimate knowledge of the business; they may even be able properly to absorb some of their fees in the annual company fees, easing the client's personal obligations. The client knows that they will be anxious to deliver a 'helpful' report; they will want to please and will hope to continue to act on behalf of the business in the future. They will also be inclined to seek to defend the client's position generally, for example by 'playing down' the share value if that is what is required, or by handling other areas of difficulty in a sympathetic way. They may also be ready to fight a rearguard action to resist closer examination of some of the less helpful paperwork, believing this to be in the client's best interests.

2.4 However, to appoint the current auditors in this situation is often a fundamental error, and very careful thought must always be given to the decision when this opportunity presents itself. There are a number of reasons for this.

(1) The perception of partisanship

2.5 The company auditors may well be seen by the other party and the court exactly as painted above, ie too fiercely loyal, self-interested, defensive, resistant to enquiry, and ultimately partisan. However professional and independent their work may eventually prove to be, the perception may be impossible to rebut, in which case the damage will be done, and the client's case will be prejudiced. Bear in mind also that disclosure of all 'material instructions' (were it to be directed) to the company auditors could be a damaging exercise.

(2) The 'too knowledgeable auditor'

2.6 The company's auditors may simply have too much knowledge of the overall business position for their own, and the client's, good. The auditors may have worked closely with the owners of the company over many years and, indeed, may have developed personal friendships with them. They may for example know too much about questionable expenses which have been funnelled through the company; the sympathetic approach adopted by the Revenue in relation to certain expenditure; the treatment of the P11D forms; a long-term plan to float the company (which is not apparent from the current position); informal offers which may have been made for purchase of shares or of the entire business in the past; the less obvious ways in which capital could be raised, etc. One always needs to be aware that, once the company auditor is in the witness-box, with a personal and professional obligation to answer honestly, clearly and comprehensively, a great deal of unexpected damage can be done. In contrast, a freshly appointed, independent accountant, working alongside the current auditors, can produce a report, give evidence, and provide enough information to satisfy the court without being vulnerable to cross-examination on matters of which he has personal knowledge, and which may cause enormous difficulties for a long-standing auditor. Furthermore, an auditor is unlikely to have the special skills possessed by a forensic accountant (as to which see below).

(3) The separation of business and personal advice

2.7 The client may not wish the company auditors to become closely involved with his or her personal matters, for all kinds of good reasons. Bear in mind that many businessmen and women already instruct separate financial advisers for business and personal matters, as a general principle.

2.8 It is always possible that the other party and their advisers will want to involve the auditors; certainly they may seek access to files, but these can generally be provided in a controlled way. If the auditors are faced with meetings and enquiries, it is important to ensure they are fully briefed but cautious in their responses. The specialist forensic accountant, determined to obtain information and experienced at negotiating agreed findings, is capable of overwhelming an inexperienced opposite number and producing an 'agreed report' which does not give an entirely fair picture. It will be the solicitor's role to assess this risk and protect against it.

2.9 A decision not to appoint the existing auditors need not be seen as an effort to hide information, or keep someone out of the witness-box. The requirements to provide information must always be respected, but the appointment of an independent specialist forensic accountant would in general be seen as logical and appropriate.

2.10 However, there may be occasions, bearing in mind the constraints and guidelines referred to above, when the company auditors are the economic and sensible choice. They can provide adequate information, a satisfactory clarification of many apparently complex questions, an interpretation of paperwork which may otherwise be confusing, a summary of the company's present and future plans, an explanation of the problems and practicalities of realising funds, and of the liquidity problems that may arise and, of course, the 'broad assessment' of the value of the shareholding which may be sufficient for the court. Whilst they will not be seen as totally independent, if they handle matters well, in some cases that may not matter unduly.

2.11 Thus the choice between the auditor and the independent accountant is one that must be carefully considered. The scope and nature of the financial disputes that may arise; any potential flashpoints; the degree of animosity and distrust between the parties; the scale of the case; the possible danger zones in the evidence on both sides; the experience and standing of the auditors, are all factors which must be taken into account. Similar considerations arise when making the decision whether or not to instruct the client's personal family accountants, assuming of course that to do so would not run the risk of creating a conflict of interest for the firm.

2.12 Bear in mind also that if both parties, and the court, are seeking to appoint a single joint expert accountant, then it is unlikely that the existing company auditors would be regarded as suitable for that role. Certainly there would generally be strong arguments for resisting such an appointment. Accountants should also note the guidelines on conflict of interest highlighted in *Prince Jefri Bolkiah v KPMG (A Firm)* [1999] 2 AC 222; care must be exercised.

2.13 If expert accountants are to be retained, whether jointly or separately, as acknowledged specialists in their field, then the instructing solicitor and the client must accept from the outset, that they will not be prepared to compromise their professional standards. They will seek full disclosure of the relevant information from both the client and the auditors, and will expect the client to give the necessary authority to the auditors to ensure that they are able to have unfettered access to the relevant papers.

2.14   The accountant will need to be comfortable with the instructions he is receiving from the client and solicitors; any effort on their part to encourage undue defensiveness or selectivity, the withholding of information, or to restrict instructions generally will be met with concern. Any expert witness of repute will be concerned to ensure that his professional reputation is maintained and, if he has a particular reputation in the context of family law, he will not allow it to be risked for the sake of one case or one unreasonably demanding client.

2.15   If each party appoints an accountant then they will each look for the same professional standards in their opposite number; if it is apparent that the other party's accountant does not have the authority to disclose all the appropriate information (confirmation of which is often requested in advance of any meeting) then either further disclosure will be required, or the report will comment appropriately and the court will draw its conclusions.

BRIEFING THE EXPERT – A CHECKLIST

2.16   If the decision is taken not to instruct the auditors or the family accountant, the questions are whom to choose, and where to find them. In practice, there is simply no substitute for a satisfactory recommendation, or the experience of specialist accountants with whom one has worked in the past. If the solicitor is not familiar with an appropriate specialist forensic accountant, then he must ensure that someone is selected who is fully aware of the role he will be required to play; the accountant chosen must have experience of advising in matrimonial litigation, of reviewing Forms E, questionnaires and documents, of attending court to give evidence as an expert witness, and of working with solicitors, counsel and clients.

2.17   Professional colleagues, senior barristers, or other accountants, will all usually be happy to give appropriate recommendations. There are many forensic accountants now who promote their expertise at seminars and elsewhere, and the various directories also provide names. Do not be afraid to ask about their levels of experience or for references from other matrimonial lawyers. Ultimately, there should be no difficulty in finding somebody suitable and experienced.

2.18   There are, however, a number of matters which the instructing solicitor should bear in mind.

- Be sure that the person who is to lead the negotiations and to give evidence in court has the necessary experience, and is also directly responsible for and at least in part involved in the work of preparation and investigation. The senior personnel may well (quite properly and justifiably) delegate a certain amount of the work to juniors; one must, however, be satisfied that the witness who will be giving evidence has a detailed personal knowledge of all the information and issues on which he is to be cross-examined in court.

- Always bear in mind that the costs to be incurred will not be insignificant; be aware of the precise basis on which the accountants will be charging, for partner and more junior time. Where appropriate, set specific limits on the extent of the costs that may be incurred at various stages. Obtain the client's authority to meet the fees once the amounts are known, and as already noted, ensure that the arrangement for payment of fees is clear. The new ancillary relief procedures focus heavily on the requirement to provide up-to-date costs information.

- If a case is to be conducted under public funding, be certain that there is authority from the Legal Services Commission to incur the expense and, where appropriate, agree hourly rates and overall costs limits.

- Often a certain amount of the work can be carried out by the client, for example the collation of his own papers, the analysis of certain of his documentation, the explanation of entries on bank statements, in company accounts etc. Where this is the case, ensure that the client or someone on his behalf carries out that work, or at least make the client aware of the cost of instructing one of the professional team to do it – often many hours' work will be involved, and any cost saving will be welcome.

- Ensure that the accountants are not under-instructed. Give them a full picture of the case, explain the background history, the personalities, the tensions, the issues, the role of counsel, the history of any previous proceedings, the aspirations of the client, the steps which are considered necessary, the likely timetable, and the cost considerations and constraints. In effect, instruct them as one would counsel – ensure that they are fully briefed rather than working in isolation and lacking an appreciation of the personalities and issues.

- Without incurring unnecessary expense, make sure that the accountants remain involved throughout the running of the case; do not make the mistake of involving them only intermittently. If there is to be a conference with counsel which will involve discussion of financial issues, ensure that the accountants are invited to attend; establish with the client, with counsel and with the accountants whether it is thought necessary for them to do so, and whether the cost is justified. If there is an interlocutory financial hearing which may be relevant, ensure that they are aware of the issues and can advise appropriately; for example an application to dispute the relevance of certain questions in the questionnaire or an injunction application to freeze particular assets.

- When the directions are finalised and a timetable is prepared for experts to meet, agree issues, prepare reports etc, make sure that the accountants are kept fully informed. When a hearing date is to be fixed, consult with them on dates in advance or at least ensure that they are notified and that it is convenient for their attendance. All this sounds elementary, but it is often overlooked.

- The preparation of bundles for the court on both interlocutory and full hearings is now of vital importance and strict practice directions have of course been given in relation to the exercise. Ensure that the accountants are fully aware of the requirements, and when preparing bundles for their consideration both as expert advisers and subsequently as expert witnesses, ensure that they have the same paginated trial bundles as counsel and the court (they too will need to cross-refer), and that they have ample opportunity to liaise with the solicitor, with the client and with counsel well in advance of the hearing.

- In the course of the running of the case, consideration should be given to the role of the accountants in any negotiations. They may have a responsibility for ensuring that sufficient disclosure has been given by the client to enable the other side to evaluate an offer (especially any without prejudice or *Calderbank* offer which may have been made), or alternatively for ensuring that there is now sufficient information available from the other side properly to evaluate the offer which they have made. It is always a risk to argue *after* the event, when the issue of costs arises, that the information supplied at the time of a without prejudice or *Calderbank* offer, was inadequate and insufficient to enable an assessment of the acceptability of the offer, especially if the client's accountants were involved at the time.

- Consider whether experts will need to sit in throughout the hearing of the case, and to what extent their attendance at court is unnecessary during other stages of the proceedings; sometimes it is vital for them to hear the other party's evidence on financial issues, and of course the evidence of the other party's advisers. Equally, however, this is an expensive investment of their time and if one is taking full notes and in a position to confer after the day's events, then it may be an unnecessary expense. On the application of either party the court may order witnesses to withdraw on both sides (other than the one giving evidence) and to ensure there is no communication before further evidence is given (see *The Supreme Court Practice*, para 38/1/6). However, the practice 'does not apply and never has applied to the parties themselves or their solicitors or their expert witnesses. Those are never excluded from the court' (*Tomlinson v Tomlinson* [1980] 1 All ER 593). In rare cases, the presence of an expert witness in court is challenged, but generally the court will not support such a challenge. The real issue is more often the balance of expense against the benefit of having the expert hear other relevant evidence.

OBSERVATIONS ON THE ACCOUNTANT'S ROLE – THE COURT'S VIEW

2.19 It might be thought from what has been said above that the court, whilst willing to respect the calibre of independent evidence from accountants, can very often be sceptical about specialist accountants and the role they play. In fact, although courts have at times been critical, they have also on many occasions expressed appreciation for the work carried out by accountants in assisting the court. Two contrasting cases which were heard by the Court of Appeal within a year of each other will serve as examples of this.

2.20 In *Preston v Preston* [1982] 1 All ER 41, Ormrod LJ recognised the important role which will often be played by the accountant. He commented as follows:

'However neither party saw fit to provide evidence from an accountant or a tax consultant as to how a large capital sum could be used to maximise spending power and reduce the liability to tax. No reference was even made to annuity tables . . . It is unreasonable to expect a Judge to make calculations of this kind without expert assistance and lack of it may have led the Judge in this case to over estimate the size of the lump sum required to comply with the terms of s 25.'

2.21 *Preston* was heard before the Court of Appeal in May–June 1981. A year later, in June 1982, the same court heard *Potter v Potter* [1982] 3 All ER 321, and their conclusions included the following damning passage in the judgment from Dunn LJ, concerning the expert evidence on the company valuation:

'But this Court has said over and over again that in cases involving redistribution of capital, the one third approach is not appropriate. This case is a good example of the practical disadvantages of this approach, because in order to arrive at a figure of the proportion of one third, a global figure has to be arrived at and, where, as in this case, the husband is engaged in a one man business, that involves a valuation of the business. This is necessarily a hypothetical exercise because the only way that it can be done is for those valuing to assume that the business would be sold. That is of course the one thing which in fact is not going to happen and very rarely does happen. This case is a particularly acute example of the result of approaching these cases in this way. No fewer than four accountants were instructed to value this comparatively small business. Three of them were called to give evidence; none of them agreed as to their conclusions, which were hotly contested; there was disagreement as to the proper way in arriving at a figure of goodwill for a business of this kind; there was disagreement as to the proper figure to be attributed to a notional managerial expense, which on one theory, it was necessary to deduct before arriving at the goodwill, and there was disagreement as to whether or not the incidence of capital gains tax and other taxes was a proper deduction from the valuation of the business. We were told that the total cost of this inquiry amounted to some £12,000, the bulk of which will no doubt be payable to the accountants. At the end of the day this exercise, namely the detailed valuation of the business, is an almost wholly irrelevant consideration.'

2.22 Ormrod LJ was also less charitable to accountants than he had been in his judgment in *Preston*. He went into some detail in his criticism of the exercise which had taken place, and ultimately reflected that in his order for costs. He said:

> 'Applying the one third rule to this case would mean that the amount to be paid by the husband would depend on valuations by accountants and here, in this case, the unfortunate Judge had before him no less than four different valuations by four different accountants. The spread of the valuations ranged between £10,000 and £40,000 for the goodwill, so that it is wholly illusory to think that by using the one third rule in relation to capital any certainty is achieved. It simply exchanges one uncertainty for another and there are no indications as to which accountant is more likely to be right because the whole thing is an imaginary exercise from beginning to end.'

2.23 When dealing with the question of costs he went on to say:

> 'The problem in this case is that much of the costs have arisen as a result of the conflict over the valuation of the goodwill of the business, and we have already commented in the course of our Judgment about the relevance of that fact. The position appears to be that originally there was not a very large gap between the wife's accountants' valuation of goodwill and the husband's accountants' valuation of the goodwill so that a compromise was possible. Unfortunately the husband called in further accountants whose valuation of the goodwill was markedly different from the wife's, and that has led to a bitter dispute between them. In those circumstances it seems unreasonable that the wife should have to bear all the heavy costs of the trial, most of which has been taken up in this futile dispute between accountants. The order I would propose is that after 8th March 1982 the husband is to have his costs but the costs are to be limited to the costs of one accountant only, and that these costs will also include the costs of applying to this court for leave to appeal out of time. There is no reason why that should not have been agreed between the parties.'

2.24 A few years later in *B v B (Financial Provision)* [1990] 1 FLR 20 accountants were, to a degree, back in favour: Ward J said that:

> 'As a result of *Preston* the practice has grown up for accountants to devise a computer programme which can calculate the lump sum which, if invested on assumptions as to life expectancy, rates of inflation, return on investments, growth of capital, incidence of income tax, will produce enough to meet the recipient's needs for life.'

He was of course describing the calculations in *Duxbury v Duxbury* [1987] 1 FLR 7, originated by one of the authors of this book, Tim Lawrence. Ward J said further that, provided the calculation is accepted as being no more than a tool for the judge's use, then it was a very valuable help to him in many cases.

2.25 Following that case, the approach suggested in *Duxbury* was re-affirmed, albeit with caution, in the cases of *Gojkovic v Gojkovic* [1990] 1 FLR 140, where there was very substantial reliance upon accountants' computations and analyses, and *Vicary v Vicary* [1992] 2 FLR 271, where again the court was reliant upon accountants' evidence, but where very careful consideration was given to the basis upon which the *Duxbury* calculation should be made. The debate on the correct approach to such calculations continues in the pages of *Family Law* and elsewhere and is reflected in the regularly updated *At A Glance*; many practitioners now have their own customised models.

Chapter 3

DISCLOSURE AND PRODUCTION OF DOCUMENTS

THE CURRENT CLIMATE: CONCERNS AND CONSTRAINTS

3.1 By the very nature of the cases which fall within the ambit of this book, the process of disclosure which they will entail is likely to be a more complex and potentially controversial procedure than in many other more straightforward cases. The scope for misjudgment is considerable, and the need for care and a professional approach that much greater.

3.2 The purpose of this chapter is to provide a practical guide to extracting and collating full and relevant disclosure of information on financial issues, whilst staying within the established procedures and guidelines. There have been a number of important recent developments. Reference has already been made to the heavy judicial criticism in this area, which has grown over the last few years. Along with the very firm guidance now being provided by the senior judiciary, three other constructive developments have occurred.

3.3 First, the procedural revolution contained in the new Rules, and analysed above, will impose a discipline and focus on disclosure as never before. It is proving effective and valuable but must not be allowed to develop into an excessively restrictive constraint.

3.4 Secondly, the SFLA's *Good Practice in Family Law on Disclosure* was published in January 1996 (see the Appendix). It is a detailed and helpful practice manual which highlights many of the issues and dilemmas which face practitioners on a daily basis, and provides sound guidance on key problems such as the timing of disclosure, privilege, 'self-help', misdirected (and intercepted) privileged mail, telephone taping and tapping, entrapment, and when the practitioner should cease to act in appropriate cases. Where available, a cross-reference to the statutory or judicial authority for the guidance is provided. This guide is a valuable starting point where any doubts arise on an issue relating to disclosure, whether it be practical, procedural or ethical.

3.5 Thirdly, the much publicised Family Law Act 1996 now apparently abandoned but still the subject of heated debate, contained much that was potentially influential. The Act placed a heavy emphasis on mediation, created a procedure designed to ensure that, in the majority of cases, the divorce decree would be finalised only once other ancillary matters (including finance) had been resolved, and introduced a timetable, which together with the

mediation process and the new ancillary relief procedures was designed to
ensure a clearer focus on resolving financial issues as an intrinsic part of
divorce. It was, in the opinion of the editors, an elaborate and in certain
respects flawed piece of legislation which would, if it were ever to re-emerge,
undoubtedly, create problems. The process of drafting and introducing it was
of course a series of compromises, and it would still have to be shaped by the
results of various related pilot schemes. There is no doubt, however, that if in
due course it arrives, even in an amended form, it will have a significant impact
on the resolution of financial disputes.

THE GENERAL RULE – FULL AND FRANK DISCLOSURE

3.6   More than 15 years ago, in the case of *Livesey v Jenkins* [1985] AC 424, the
necessity of providing proper disclosure was revisited. It was reiterated that
each party owed a duty to the court to make full and frank disclosure of all
material facts to the other party, and to the court. That duty applied not just to
contested proceedings but to all exchanges of correspondence between parties
and their solicitors leading to consent orders. In the absence of complete,
correct and up-to-date information on the matters to which it was required to
have regard under s 25 of the Matrimonial Causes Act 1973, the court could not
properly exercise its discretion. It is possible that at that time this needed
restatement; but whether the issues canvassed then have been in any way
responsible for the explosion of ancillary relief costs, as identified by judge after
judge, can be only a matter of conjecture.

3.7   It is a regrettable reality that often not all relevant information and
documents are provided voluntarily either with the Form E or subsequently as a
result of enquiry by questionnaire. There are a number of additional methods
which must be considered by practitioners to obtain the necessary information
and in this chapter we deal with the options available.

3.8   Some documents are available as public records; the best example,
particularly relevant here, is the company file at Companies House, but there
are others such as land registry title details, trade mark and patent information
and certain public sector salary scales and pension information, although these
will be of limited use.

3.9   The new Rules have removed the original 'catch all' provisions of r 2.63 of
the Family Proceedings Rules 1991 (FPR 1991) which provided that:

> 'Any party to an application for ancillary relief may by letter require any other party
> to give further information concerning any matter contained in any Affidavit filed
> by or on behalf of that other party, or any other relevant matter, or to furnish a list
> of relevant documents or to allow inspection of any such document, and may, in
> default of compliance by such other party, apply to the District Judge for
> directions.'

These issues must now be dealt with in the Form E, or at the First Appointment or after the FDR, but not on an *ad hoc* basis, as they often were previously.

3.10   There is the rather rarer route of the Bankers' Books Evidence Act 1879 and there is the more conventional route of the production appointment under r 2.62(7) of the FPR 1991. Each of these is dealt with below.

A warning to practitioners

3.11   Although it has largely been overtaken by the new Rules, the President's *Practice Direction: Case Management* (31 January 1995) [1995] 1 FLR 456, which dealt forcefully with the issues of delay and costs still sounds a warning note. It is reproduced in full in the Appendix. The direction made very clear the determination within the Family Division to ensure that cases were conducted economically, and warned of costs (and wasted costs) orders in the event of failure. The court would exercise discretion to limit disclosure, and would expect the duty of full and frank disclosure to be respected. Additionally, it specifically required the parties and their advisers to use their best endeavours 'to reduce or eliminate issues for expert evidence'. Those responsibilities now fall more directly upon the court under the new procedures, but every practitioner needs to be aware of the standards which are set, and to ensure that they are maintained.

MATTERS OF PUBLIC RECORD

Company accounts

3.12   Unlike almost any other asset which is the subject of disclosure in matrimonial proceedings, there is a good deal of information concerning a company incorporated in the UK which can be gleaned from documents which are a matter of public record. These can be examined fully before any further enquiries are raised, and it may be sensible to do so.

3.13   All companies registered in England and Wales must provide information about themselves to the Companies Registry in Cardiff. Scottish companies must do the same to their registry in Edinburgh. Overseas companies with a branch or place of business in the UK must also provide information about themselves to the Companies Registry in Cardiff. All information provided to these Companies Registries is available for public inspection.

3.14   The following documents and information must be filed and should be available:

(a)   Memorandum and Articles of Association and any changes;
(b)   certificate of incorporation and notice of change of name;
(c)   details of directors, secretary and registered office and all changes to those details;

(d)   details of issue of shares and changes to share capital;

(e)   charges register, identifying secured creditors and assets charged;

(f)   annual returns filed once a year with up-to-date details of the registered office, members, directors, secretary and share capital;

(g)   annual accounts filed in respect of every financial year of the company (generally many months behind).

3.15   These documents will give a helpful outline picture of the company, its directors, their other directorships, shareholders, share capital, mortgages and general financial position. However, it is important to note that because of the regulations governing the filing of accounts, the information on the company file can often be many months out of date. A private company has up to 10 months after its year end to supply its accounts. Read the accounts carefully to ascertain the period to which they refer, the date they were signed and the filing date; this will also give some insight into how efficiently the company finances are run. It is frequently necessary to ask in your questionnaire for more recent draft accounts and management accounts for the intervening period, and (if one is appointed by then) to liaise with the accountant to consider whether the company information you now have is sufficiently up to date and comprehensive.

3.16   In the case of a larger company, check that the accounts have been audited by independent accountants who have reported that they represent a true and fair view of the affairs of the company. If there are qualifications, be certain to understand their purpose and significance. In the case of companies with a turnover not greater than £2.8 million, total assets not greater than £1.4 million and not more than 50 employees, it is possible that only abbreviated accounts consisting solely of a balance sheet will be filed, and these are likely to be inadequate for the purposes of the investigation. It is the profit and loss accounts and the notes to them which could provide information about dividends declared and remuneration paid to directors.

3.17   Beware also that, in the case of smaller companies, the information available may be less reliable. For accounting periods ending on or before 15 June 1997, if the turnover was under £90,000, an audit by accountants was not necessary at all; if it was between £90,000 and £350,000, then only a lesser form of report was required from accountants stating that the company accounts are in accordance with its accounting records. For accounting periods ending after 15 June 1997, no audit is required for companies with turnover below £350,000 and total assets of not more than £1.4 million and a full audit for companies with turnover or assets above these thresholds.

3.18   Thus, although the filed accounts will provide some historical information concerning the financial standing of the company, and possibly dividends declared and the remuneration of the directors, they may be far from adequate for providing either a complete or an up-to-date picture. Substantial additional information and more rigorous investigation could be needed.

3.19   A good deal of the initial work in this area can be carried out by the solicitor, or indeed by the client. The Internet has widened the options hugely, and agencies will provide company searches usually within a day or two, or even on the same day. Searches can be made in person at the Companies Registry if necessary (there are offices in Cardiff, London, Edinburgh, Birmingham, Manchester, Leeds and Glasgow) and it is also possible to arrange for Companies House to provide information by post or fax direct, or to be connected to their records via a PC for the purpose of on-line searches.

3.20   When bespeaking a search, the following details at least should be requested:

- full name, number, registered office, date of incorporation;
- copy accounts and annual returns for the past three years, with details of any changes to directors and secretary and share capital since last return;
- unregistered charges;
- Memorandum and Articles of Association (especially if share transfers or removal of directors is in issue);
- details of appointments of any liquidator or receiver.

Where appropriate, a copy of the search can be obtained on microfiche and the full details of the file researched on a fiche reader. It is possible to search against names of directors for lists of all their directorships.

3.21   Some agencies will also produce more detailed 'credit' or 'status' reports which will provide not simply the information on the company searches but some form of analysis of the company's financial position, details of county court judgments, and any public information which may be available in the case of larger companies; although such reports are intended more for the use of potential suppliers or customers. In addition, experienced enquiry agents and commercial investigators may also be able to unearth information not readily available elsewhere.

3.22   Also, the Internet can be very valuable for accessing not simply company search details but a wide range of international commercial information.

See further the section below (paras **3.46** *et seq*) concerning compelling production of other company documents (*B v B (Matrimonial Proceedings: Discovery)* [1978] Fam 181).

OFFSHORE SEARCHES

3.23   Although all companies registered in England and Wales must provide information about themselves to the Companies Registry in Cardiff, and Scottish companies likewise do so to the Registry in Edinburgh, you may also need to obtain information concerning overseas companies. In the case of companies with no link to the UK some jurisdictions have centralised companies registries, especially those systems based on English law, for example, Hong Kong and Canada. The UK, however, is unusual in that here company accounts are filed; this may well not be the case elsewhere.

3.24 A possible first enquiry may be to search agents in UK, some of whom have correspondents overseas and can advise on information likely to be available. A second enquiry may best be made to a local lawyer or accountant. The Appendix includes helpful summaries of the sources of offshore company information in certain jurisdictions.

LAND REGISTRY SEARCHES

3.25 Now that the Land Register is open, title searches, where the land in question can be thoroughly identified, may prove helpful, and can provide, in addition to ownership details, plans, previous owners, subsisting and cancelled charges, all of which may be relevant.

PREPARING QUESTIONNAIRES – A CHECKLIST

3.26 Whilst these lines of enquiry referred to above represent a first step in the investigation of a business which is a limited company, and can be taken with minimum expense to the client, the scope of the investigation is likely to remain modest unless further documentation is obtained to ensure that a full and accurate picture of the business is presented. Additionally, of course, many businesses are not incorporated. Documentation will then have to be requested from the other party generally by means of a questionnaire which will in turn require the court seal of approval; other lines of enquiry may also be pursued. The request for business-related information is likely to include at least some of the following, depending upon the nature of the case:

- full audited accounts including profit and loss accounts;
- management accounts prepared since the last audited accounts whether on a quarterly or monthly basis;
- draft audited accounts if these have not yet been finalised or approved but are in the process of being so;
- recent valuations of properties where appropriate and justified (see Chapter 5, para **5.16**);
- P11Ds setting out the expenses claimed by directors in the course of business;
- details of directors' loan accounts, and all drawings which may not be shown in the audited accounts;
- company bank statements from the company bank accounts;
- company credit card statements;

- correspondence between the company, its tax advisers and the Inland Revenue where unpaid tax or likely tax computations are in issue;
- copies of transaction files relating either to the purchase or sale of the company or related companies or parts of the business or of company assets, or their proposed purchase or sale;
- directors' service contracts and shareholder or partnership agreements where relevant to the party's income, capital or liquidity position;
- share option arrangements or incentive schemes;
- shareholder loan documents;
- company pension schemes and all related documentation and correspondence with pension advisers and with the Inland Revenue.

3.27 It will be apparent from the potential scale of these enquiries that the reaction of the court must be carefully considered. The cost of identifying what is needed, and requesting this information, is likely to be considerable, and will add a burden to the overall cost of litigation which in turn will reduce the amount of the family assets. The principle of proportionality will underpin the court's decision, and cost-effectiveness and genuine justification, linked directly to the issues in the case, will be fundamental concerns. It is therefore important that a clear picture as to what is genuinely necessary is formed and developed as the investigation proceeds. This requires co-operation between solicitor and accountant to ensure that nothing is overlooked, but also that no unnecessary information is demanded. Chapter 8 below, 'The Husband's Hidden Wealth', deals with some of the more specific questions which may be raised where there is concern about the accuracy or completeness of the disclosure provided and a genuine need to investigate more rigorously.

3.28 Enquiries may not be made piecemeal. The questionnaire should be carefully drafted and focused, not simply taken without thought from the word processor. Where appropriate, there should be consultation with specialist counsel. It is vital that the costs of discovery do not become disproportionate to the extent of the information sought, and to the value of the assets involved in the case. Equally, however, a well constructed questionnaire will uncover gaps or inconsistencies in the evidence already presented, and in doing so will put pressure on any party who has failed to disclose thoroughly, or who is unwilling to do so, and may increase their inclination to make sensible settlement proposals.

3.29 Finally, bear in mind the Court of Appeal decision in *Baker v Baker* [1995] 2 FLR 829, which reviews the court's right to draw adverse inferences from a failure to provide full and frank disclosures. It was held that, on the facts of that case, the judge was entitled to draw inferences adverse to the husband, having found as a fact that the husband had deliberately concealed his true position. The judgment of Butler-Sloss LJ makes salutary reading on these issues.

INTERROGATORIES

3.30 The case of *Hildebrand v Hildebrand* [1992] 1 FLR 244, heard in December 1990, predated even the previous Rules, but in it Waite J dealt helpfully with the relationship between the questionnaire (then under Matrimonial Causes Rules 1977, r 77(4)) and interrogatories. He stated:

> 'A questionnaire partakes of the character both of a request for discovery and of an interrogatory, since it may require an answer to questions of fact or seek production of documents or both.'

He considered the then new interrogatory procedure order, Rules of the Supreme Court 1965, Ord 26, enabling the service of interrogatories without leave, and without deciding the point, was prepared to assume that the new procedure prevailed in the Family Division.

3.31 The circumstances of *Hildebrand* were complex and unusual, involving, in part, the question of whether the husband, who had obtained a substantial number of the wife's documents improperly, should therefore be disentitled to demand answers to his questionnaire and interrogatories. In summary, Waite J concluded that it was clear:

> 'from the unreported Court of Appeal decisions in *Arora v Goole* and *Arora v Pheby* that interrogatories will not be allowed to provide a party with the means of some form of roving cross-examination before trial.'

He went on to decide that the husband should not be entitled to interrogate or procure his questionnaire, given his behaviour in taking discovery into his own hands. He also concluded that in any event the husband's interrogatories were 'wide-ranging and oppressive', including 51 questions, and were 'a classic example of the oppressive interrogatory which was excluded under the old procedure'. 'Interrogatories', he added, quoting the *Supreme Court Practice* side note 26/1/4/e, 'will not be allowed if they exceed the legitimate requirements of the particular occasion'.

3.32 In *Hall v Sevalco Ltd* [1996] PIQR P344, the court refused to order interrogatories which were not necessary, stressing that orders for discovery, interrogatories, replies to questionnaires under the FPR 1991, r 2.63, orders for production of documents etc are all matters for the court's discretion. The key word is 'necessary' and if necessity cannot be established the application will fail. Fishing expeditions will not be allowed.

3.33 Note that the party receiving the interrogatories is required to answer them on affidavit, unless otherwise ordered, and whether they are served under order or not. The sanction for not replying may be a strike out or an application for committal.

3.34 In most cases now, under the new Rules, any interrogatory-style questions will be raised in questionnaires, and again it is for the district judge to decide upon their legitimacy; are they a roving cross-examination before trial, or are they raising further relevant questions necessary to ensure full and frank disclosure?

DIRECTIONS ORDERS

3.35 As already noted, the standard directions on expert evidence will often involve requirements that experts meet well in advance of the hearing, consider what areas of dispute there may be, prepare appropriate reports and identify areas of disagreement. This procedure should be carried out against the background of such disclosure as is necessary to achieve satisfactory results. Further enquiries may have to be made as the case develops, and leave may be needed for a further questionnaire.

3.36 Practitioners will be aware that if such issues arise either as to the extent of the disclosure that is sought, or as to the relevance of the questions in the questionnaire, or if the adequacy of the answers is challenged, or answers are simply not produced, then the matter can and should be referred back to a district judge who will make an appropriate ruling and a costs award as necessary. Under the new procedure this will most likely be at the conclusion of the FDR once it becomes clear that settlement is unlikely, or in the few weeks prior to the final hearing as the issues crystallise and/or updating more detailed information becomes necessary. If there is any doubt as to whether aspects of the information produced by the questionnaire will ultimately be of value, then the district judge may make an order requiring the disclosure, but leaving the question of costs at risk until the final hearing. In some cases, it is only at that stage that an assessment can be made of the need for that particular disclosure and the justification for seeking it. Alternatively, an order may be refused in relation to any part of the questionnaire, if the conclusion is that the information requested is simply not sufficiently relevant.

3.37 As suggested above, the appointed accountants should generally have an input into the drafting of a questionnaire or the preparation of the answers to it. If they are to be requested to carry out a business valuation, even of the broadest nature, then it should be ensured that they have all the information and documents they reasonably need.

INSPECTION APPOINTMENTS AND CONSEQUENT INVESTIGATIONS

3.38 Where the party under investigation is effectively the '*alter ego*' of the company, then it may be possible to obtain an order for inspection of the company's bank account under s 5(7) of the Bankers' Books Evidence Act 1879. Paid cheques and paying-in slips are not within the definition of 'bankers' books' and are not disclosable. They may be obtainable under an inspection appointment and (especially if it is not possible to obtain annotated bank statements) can often be extremely revealing, and most helpful in painting an accurate and more comprehensive picture of the family expenditure patterns than will otherwise be available. Bank records too can be extremely useful. Quite often they will include attendance notes of meetings or telephone discussions, details of transactions undertaken, financial details disclosed informally by the customer, etc.

DISCLOSURE OF BANKS' INTERNAL RECORDS

3.39 A recent decision of the High Court Chancery Division, *In re Howglen Ltd* LTL, 10 April 2000, reinforces the limited obligation of banks to produce copy documents under the Bankers' Books Evidence Act 1879 but lays banks open to orders for disclosure of documents even though they are not party to the proceedings in question.

The case involved a director fighting disqualification proceedings under the Company Directors Disqualification Act 1986, where the principal allegation was that he caused his company to trade whilst insolvent. He denied that his bank manager had advised him at a meeting that the company was insolvent, and was initially successful in obtaining a very wide order under the 1879 Act, for the production to him of all notes taken by the bank manager of meetings with the director in the relevant period, together with other notes and even the bank's internal memoranda. On appeal, however, the High Court held that the obligation in the 1879 Act was restricted to records similar to ledgers, day books, cash books and account books, ie the means by which the bank records its day-to-day financial transactions.

Nevertheless the judge in that case also felt that it was important that the director had a proper opportunity to defend himself and that he should have access to bank documents provided that they were relevant and identifiable. The route he adopted was to use part of the CPR 1998 enabling courts to order a non-party to litigation to disclose documents if they are likely to support the case of one party to the proceedings (in this case the director) or adversely affect the case of the other party. The judge ordered the bank to disclose specific documents and specific categories of documents which met this test including, in particular, their notes of important meetings with the director. He warned, however, against using this procedure as a fishing expedition against banks.

This case could well have implications for the disclosure of important bank internal records in the context of matrimonial proceedings, perhaps in evaluating the husband's relationship with the bank, for example in connection with borrowing facilities; the future success of his company; the possibility of expansion, flotation, merger, acquisition etc.

3.40 The more conventional approach now is to pursue an inspection appointment under r 2.62(7) of the FPR 1991. This is a procedure whereby *any party* may apply to the court for an order that *any person* attend an appointment (an 'inspection appointment') before the court and produce the documents specified in the order. The documents must appear to the court to be necessary for disposing fairly of the application for ancillary relief or for saving costs. No-one shall be required to produce a document at an inspection appointment which they could not be compelled to produce at the hearing of the application for ancillary relief. Inspection appointments are not exactly a new concept; they simply bring forward to a preliminary hearing the *subpoena duces tecum*, which was often the cause of delay and increased costs, as under the previous jurisdiction documents were only produced at the final hearing. Under the present procedure, documents can be made available well ahead of the trial, saving costs, possibly prompting settlement, and avoiding delays in the hearing whilst they are belatedly added to the trial bundle and the hearing is adjourned for them to be read. The FPR 1991 provide for the person ordered to attend to have representation. Copies of documents may be taken only by agreement.

Checklist of significant points when considering an inspection appointment

3.41 The FPR 1991 do not contain much detail but the move to increased case management by district judges will assist in ensuring that the main directions as to disclosure are given at an early stage in the process, and carefully and clearly defined. If this works effectively, then the need for inspection appointments may diminish. Under the FPR 1991 (r 2.62(7)), this process was labelled a 'production' appointment and thus the case references use this phrase. There is no reason to suppose that the principles deriving from those cases are no longer applicable.

- Generally, the application for leave will be made to the district judge in chambers, with an affidavit in support which must set out the nature of the proceedings, the relevance of the documents to the proceedings and their necessity; this application must usually be made on notice to the other party, rather than *ex parte*, and not at that stage to the third party; this will enable the court to 'weed out' unnecessary or oppressive applications.

- It may, on rare occasions, be appropriate to apply *ex parte* if there is a genuine and justifiable anxiety that the giving of notice may lead to destruction or disappearance of the documents sought (*B v B (No 2) (Production Appointment: Procedure)* [1995] 1 FLR 913).

- The application must also identify carefully those documents which are sought and the time period of the enquiry. Note the case of *Frary v Frary and Another* [1993] 2 FLR 696 (see paras **3.32** and **3.73**) which deal with vital issues of disclosure by a wealthy cohabiting partner of one of the parties, and considered the justification for extracting evidence from that partner.

– When leave is obtained to issue the application (generally from the district judge) it must be served on the third party, requiring them to attend on a return date and to state whether or not they are willing to produce the documents requested.

– The application should be issued in good time before the hearing.

– A third party is entitled to separate representation.

– No 'fishing expeditions' for information which is not clearly defined will be permitted.

– Costs orders will always be made as appropriate, and may cover advice, the representation and copying charges, and may well be made on an indemnity basis in favour of an unimpeachable third party.

– There is no ground to refuse an application, save where it can be agreed that it represents an unnecessary invasion of the third party's right to privacy, or on the usual basis pertaining to privilege. The court will have to balance the interests of the parties to the litigation with the interests and privacy of third parties; the test set out in *Morgan* (see para **3.83** below).

– If required, there will generally be a further appointment when the documents are produced.

The exercise of the court's discretion on inspection appointments: some examples

3.42   The case of *Frary*, mentioned above, raises other issues concerning inspection appointments. In that case, the principle of r 2.62(8) of the FPR 1991, which provides that no one can be compelled to produce documents which they could not be required to produce at a hearing, was invoked; it was concluded that the husband's co-habitee was not obliged to disclose documents dealing with his financial affairs, as the wife had stated that she did not require the co-habitee's attendance at the final hearing. In addition, the court held that the relevance of the disclosure was minimal, and that ordering production would be 'oppressive and unnecessary'.

Ralph Gibson LJ said:

> 'The task of this court in the exercise of its discretion is to balance the interests of the petitioner in obtaining the information against the interests and wishes of the third party not to divulge it.'

He went on to stress that the new procedure in the FPR 1991 did not alter the principles upon which production would be ordered, it merely brought forward the time for disclosure. He concluded that: 'if the court would issue a subpoena duces tecum or make an order for the production of documents at trial, it can make that order for production at a production appointment under the rule'.

3.43   The limitations of the process, as they emerge from *Frary*, are that it is available only for production of documents, and only those documents which could have been compelled to be produced at the final hearing. The relevance of the disclosure is also clearly a factor, and the balancing of the interests of the competing parties is an important discretionary exercise which the court will treat seriously. Under the new Rules, the principle of proportionality will also be applied.

3.44   In *D v D (Production Appointment)* [1995] 2 FLR 497, Thorpe J dealt with other issues which went beyond simply the question of inspection appointments. In an application in ancillary relief proceedings, the husband on a production summons sought disclosure of information about his wife's finances from his father-in-law's accountant, and the application was granted and backdated a number of years to cover a key period in the restructuring of the wife's family's finances. This case raises issues of professional privilege and the extent to which the court could override such privilege in the pursuit of disclosure, and it encourages the broader approach to disclosure in cases where manifest evidence of a lack of full and frank disclosure can be inferred.

3.45   Commentators have noted that, in the Chancery Division case of *Khanna v Lovell White Durrant (A Firm)* [1995] 1 WLR 121, Sir Donald Nicholls V-C decided that there was discretion to order production of documents in advance of the trial despite the defendant firm's objection to doing so prior to the hearing of the main issue. Whether this approach will extend to the issue (without leave) of Family Division subpoenas or county court witness summonses remains to be seen, but it could herald a development in this area.

OBTAINING DISCLOSURE OF COMPANY AND PARTNERSHIP DOCUMENTS

3.46   When one of the parties is in effect the '*alter ego*' of a company by virtue of having unfettered control of it, he or she may not hide behind the corporate veil. In certain cases, as for example *B v B (Matrimonial Proceedings: Discovery)* [1978] Fam 181, a party (in that case, the husband) may be required to produce, inter alia, all the account books, private ledgers, paid cheques, cheque stubs, and all documents and vouchers of the company, relating to bills and expenses incurred by the party or the company, and records of all money received by the company in the course of trading over a specified period.

3.47   The order in the case was made by a district judge and upheld on appeal by Dunn J. He concluded that the court had a discretion to order disclosure of documents which were in the possession, custody or power of the other party to the suit. Accordingly, company documents which were relevant to the matters in issue in the litigation, although in the legal possession of the company, might be required to be disclosed by a director of the company who was party to the suit, if they were or had been in his actual possession albeit as a servant or agent of the company. Whether the company documents were within the director's control was a question of fact which depended on the extent of his shareholding, the view of the company board and its constitution generally, and any objections which may be lodged. Dunn J concluded that the court's discretion to order production of those documents would be exercised by balancing the relevance and importance of the documents and the hardship likely to be caused to the other party by their non-production, against any prejudice which might be caused to the other party or to third parties such as directors and other shareholders if an order for production was made. The case makes it clear that it was not the court's practice to order production of company documents where the board of the company objected on affidavit to their production, provided that the objection was not contrived to frustrate the court's jurisdiction.

3.48 Although in an application by a wife for financial provision, disclosure of audited accounts together with full disclosure of the husband's financial records might generally be sufficient, in some cases the court would go behind the company's accounts and order specific disclosure. In this case, the documents relating to the husband's entertainment and travel expenses and his expenditure on his family were relevant to the application before the court, had been in the husband's custody, should be disclosed, and subject to any objection to their production, should be produced for inspection.

3.49 The same principles would, it is submitted, be applicable to the disclosure of partnership information, where one partner would generally have access to all the relevant documents, but other partners might take exception to uncontrolled and arguably inappropriate disclosure. The court would be willing to exercise discretion sympathetically provided the objections were valid and properly motivated. It would be anxious to establish that any objection was not simply prompted by or on behalf of the objecting spouse for unacceptable reasons. If, ultimately, a spouse will not disclose, on the basis that documents are not in his power, custody or control and/or because his co-directors or partners refuse to allow him to do so, an application must be made to a third party for an inspection appointment, and the decision will be made by the district judge.

THE MILLIONAIRE'S DEFENCE TO DISCLOSURE: IS IT STILL APPLICABLE AFTER *WHITE*?

3.50 A line of argument, expressed in articles, and deriving also from case-law, has developed in respect of certain cases, where the advisers acting for one party, taking a defensive stance in relation to thorough investigation, have maintained that the client is sufficiently wealthy to meet any financial award the court will make, and that there is, therefore, no purpose in pursuing detailed investigations, or providing lengthy disclosure. Whilst there has been considerable judicial sympathy with the theory behind this approach, it does not excuse an obligation to provide at the very least a basic level of disclosure (even if it is not accompanied by very much documentation). Nor is it applicable merely to millionaires.

3.51   It has been suggested, to use the popular expression, that a 'big money case' is one in which joint assets exceed £1.5 million. However, to justify the 'millionaire's defence', after a long marriage, it is more likely that the court would require the minimum figure to be nearer £15–20 million. Even at this level of wealth, the party invoking such a defence has been obliged to state in broad general terms (to the nearest million perhaps?) the amount of his total wealth, and to provide a schedule showing how that amount is calculated.

3.52   In *Van G v Van G (Financial Provision: Millionaires' Defence)* [1995] 1 FLR 328, the husband acknowledged in his affidavit that his total net worth was in excess of £10 million and contended that disclosure was unnecessary as he could meet any order the court might make in favour of the wife. He also argued that, given the wife's own assets, there was unlikely to be an order in her favour in any event.

3.53   Ewbank J found that in order to comply with s 25 of the Matrimonial Causes Act 1973, the court needed a minimum of information, and that the husband's submission was not sufficient. He concluded:

> 'So far as capital is concerned, I propose to make an order that he should give a summary of all assets worth more than £100,000, with an approximate estimated value of each asset, but without any supporting evidence. If that can be done on a single sheet of paper, so much the better.
>
> So far as income is concerned, the court under s 25 has to have regard to the income of the husband. He has given no details whatsoever. The size of his income goes directly to the standard of living which he could enjoy, and I accordingly think that he should give an estimate of his total income as well.
>
> If there are any pension rights which the wife is going to lose on divorce, she is at the very least entitled to know what she has lost, and I make an order that he is to give a statement of any pension rights that she has so lost.'

3.54   The same approach was adopted by Thorpe J in *F v F* (see para **1.40**), when he concluded that whilst the husband's wealth brought him within the ambit of the millionaire's defence, he would still be expected to answer reasonable questions intended to establish the broad realities of the case and shed light on past dealings. It is clear that the court will continue to require a broad outline of the husband's financial position, even in these cases.

3.55   In *Dart v Dart* [1996] 2 FLR 286, Peter Gibson L J was less persuaded of the merits of the millionaire's defence. In his judgment, he commented:

> 'Looking at the statutory provision in the absence of authority and leaving aside those provisions which relate to children, I observe first that by s 25(1) a duty is imposed on the court in deciding whether to make a property adjustment order to

have regard to all the circumstances of the case. That could not be wider. By s 25(2) regard is in particular to be had to matters included in the eight lettered paragraphs. Paragraph (a) includes "the . . . property and other financial resources which each of the parties to the marriage has". That to my mind casts doubts on the correctness of an approach in a "big money" case that treats as immaterial the actual amount of the property and other financial resources of the respondent once it is shown that they are sufficient to meet the reasonable requirements of the applicant. Paragraph (b) refers to the financial needs, obligations and responsibilities which each of the parties has or is likely to have in the foreseeable future. An approach which determines the quantum of the award by reference only to the reasonable requirements of the applicant again seems to me to be arguably incorrect.'

This judgment foreshadows the approach which has now been adopted in *White* and, together with that case, goes some way towards driving a nail or two into the coffin of the millionaire's defence. In *White* (see Chapter 1), the court placed much less emphasis on 'reasonable requirements' and far more weight on 'the yardstick of equality'. In this context, it will clearly be essential for the court to understand fully the extent of the family assets – their nature and value; their source; the degree of liquidity; the contribution from the parties in relation to each of them, in order to enable it to consider the fair division. The broadbrush approach inherent in the millionaire's defence will not survive this rigorous analysis, save perhaps in short marriage cases, where there has been little contribution from one party, and where a modest capital settlement is the inevitable outcome.

THE USE OF INJUNCTIONS, *MAREVA* INJUNCTIONS AND *ANTON PILLER* ORDERS

3.56   Injunctions may be used effectively within matrimonial proceedings, for a number of purposes. Most commonly they are invoked to frustrate or prevent a disposition which may be designed to defeat a claim for financial relief, whether under s 37 of the Matrimonial Causes Act 1973, through the use of a *Mareva* injunction (also known as a freezing injunction), or arguably by virtue of the inherent jurisdiction of the court. An application for an *Anton Piller* order (also known as a search order), enabling the applicant to enter premises and search for and seize material documents, may also be available in a very limited number of cases.

Matrimonial Causes Act 1973, section 37

3.57   The general criterion that must be satisfied is that one party is about to make a disposition designed to defeat or frustrate the other party's financial claims on divorce; s 37(2) gives the court power to make orders to prevent or set aside dispositions designed to defeat a claim for financial relief.

3.58   The application may be brought within the High Court or the county court jurisdiction. It must be made in accordance with r 2.68 of the FPR 1991.

3.59   The application will usually be made ex parte, and the applicant must prepare both an affidavit in support of the application and a draft of the order sought. Once the order is obtained, a return date will be given for an inter partes hearing, and the summons must be issued before the return date.

3.60   An ex parte applicant must, in particular:

(a)   make *full* disclosure of all material facts including evidence against him or her and possible defences which may be raised by the respondent in the application;

(b)   before making the application, make additional enquiries to ascertain any relevant facts which may have some bearing on the necessity for injunctive relief; a failure to do so could equate to a material non-disclosure. In *Brinks-Matt Limited v Elcombe* [1988] 3 All ER 188, it was held that not only facts which were known to the applicant, but also any additional facts which the applicant would have known had he made enquiries, will determine whether or not there has been material non-disclosure. The extent of the requisite enquiries will depend upon the circumstances of the case, including the nature of the applicant's case and the probable effect of the order upon the defendant.

Mareva injunctions

3.61   It has been successfully argued that the court may grant a *Mareva* injunction even where the criteria of s 37 are not fulfilled; in short, if it appears that it would be just or convenient to do so. Although in commercial cases (especially extra-territorial applications) the requirements are stringent, in matrimonial cases the courts appear in practice to take a more flexible approach, although the present position is not entirely clear. Generally speaking, if the applicant can establish a claim for a share of the relevant asset which is the subject of the application, and/or can demonstrate a serious risk of dissipation, illustrated, for example, by the respondent's past conduct, or where he is not prepared to give undertakings, then the order will be granted. To establish a reasonable case in an extra-territorial application, it will be necessary to demonstrate that there are insufficient assets located within the jurisdiction to satisfy the applicant's financial claims.

3.62   In the case of *Shipman v Shipman* [1991] 1 FLR 250, the court rejected an argument that the safeguards and restrictions on the use of worldwide *Mareva* injunctions in the commercial field should be applied within the matrimonial field. The Registrar had ordered the injunction pursuant to s 37; on appeal to Lincoln J, he concluded that there was no evidence of an intention to defeat the wife's claim, and thus a s 37 injunction was not possible. However, he held that the court had an inherent jurisdiction to make the order. He took the view that, notwithstanding the current good intentions of the respondent and the lack of any evidence that he intended to defeat the petitioner's claim through disposal of his assets, the extra-territorial injunction should be continued on the basis that the respondent might alter his intentions. In that case the husband had already given very considerable disclosure, had always maintained the wife and had kept her informed as to what he intended to do with the lump sum he was to receive. None of this was apparently sufficient to satisfy Lincoln J that he might not change his intentions at a future date.

3.63 It seems a harsh decision, and there has been some debate amongst commentators as to whether *Shipman* remains good law. *Ghoth v Ghoth* [1992] 2 All ER 920 has already overturned certain aspects of *Shipman* and has been reinforced by a Practice Direction on the granting of *Mareva* injunctions which applies in all three divisions of the High Court; see [1994] 2 FLR 704. It is now confirmed that the instructions and safeguards surrounding *Mareva* injunctions must be included in Family Division *Mareva* orders; this runs contrary to the opinion expressed by Lincoln J in *Shipman*, who advocated 'a different approach' in the matrimonial field.

3.64 The court's jurisdiction to make extra-territorial orders does not stem from any authority over the foreign assets; it is an authority exercisable in person against the respondent and the court's ability to enforce the order will in the last resort rest on the use of its coercive powers against the respondent. Ultimately, the efficacy of the sanction of the order will rest upon whether or not the court of the foreign locus will recognise and enforce the order. It is only through such recognition and enforcement that the order will be capable of binding a third party such as a bank and preventing it from assisting the respondent in asset dissipation.

3.65 *Ghoth v Ghoth* (see above) is also the authority for the fact that the court will not grant either party in matrimonial proceedings a *Mareva* injunction which extends to *all* the assets of the other party, even subject to the usual exceptions. It argues that the purpose of the injunction is to safeguard the applicant from a situation in which assets are dissipated by the respondent, with the intention of making that party 'judgment-proof', or in which, without reasonable excuse, that is the effect of dealing with the assets. As it is extremely unlikely, in matrimonial proceedings, that an applicant would be awarded the whole of the respondent's assets, attempting to obtain an order covering all assets would not be a realistic approach to adopt.

The inherent jurisdiction of the court

3.66 Lincoln J in *Shipman*, citing a number of supporting cases, maintained that the court has an inherent jurisdiction to make asset-freezing orders, and that it would do so in cases where the s 37 criteria are not fulfilled. Some commentators have, as mentioned above, questioned this, and have challenged the approach adopted in *Shipman*. It would seem that the preferred and sounder approach is likely to be an application under s 37.

Anton Piller Orders

3.67 The *Anton Piller* order, an ex parte interlocutory injunction available to an applicant under which he or she may enter the respondent's premises and search for and seize material documents and articles, can from time to time be usefully applied in matrimonial proceedings where the court deems it appropriate. It may be a helpful remedy, for example, in situations where one of the parties is still employed by or is the director of a small company, where there is fear that assets may be transferred between the business partners or to another separate but convenient company, thereby gaining an advantage in reducing or avoiding claims for financial relief. However, extreme caution should be exercised in the use of such applications.

3.68 In *Emanuel v Emanuel* [1982] 2 All ER 342, it was held that since the husband was clearly ready to flout the authority of the court and mislead it if it were to his advantage to do so, and since there was a grave danger that the documents sought by the wife would be destroyed, she should be granted the order sought. It was, said Wood J, an exceptional case; the husband had disposed of assets, ignored court orders and already been committed for contempt. The criteria to be satisfied were as follows:

(a) the applicant must establish a very strong prima facie case that the documentation is relevant, has not been produced and will not be produced without the order;

(b) there is a grave danger that evidence will be destroyed before any inter partes hearing;

(c) the respondent must have in his or her possession the relevant material.

There is a useful precedent of Wood J's order in the case report.

3.69 The applicant's duty in an *Anton Piller* case extends to making full disclosure in affidavit in support of the application, including making sufficient enquiries. The arguments for both sides must be put fairly, dealing with all points both for and against, ultimately satisfying the court that the case meets all the above criteria and, if it is appropriate, that the applicant would be able to meet any sums due upon the required cross-undertaking as to damages. The draft orders are available in standard form; it is, however, essential that the proper precedent is prepared by the applicant and that the order is executed absolutely in accordance with the required procedures, which are complex and stringent.

3.70 The court places extreme weight on the execution of the order in a proper fashion and on the fact that the solicitor involved is acting as an officer of the court. An *Anton Piller* order will not provide any right to force entry to the premises and in the event of refusal, an application for committal will have to be made.

3.71 The application for and execution of an *Anton Piller* order is a complex operation, and one should be sought and executed only with a thorough understanding of the practice involved. The following should always be borne in mind:

– that it is an expensive procedure in costs and time;
– that the order cannot be used as a 'fishing expedition' in establishing the case the applicant intends to pursue;
– that the application is made at the risk of the applicant as to costs, as even if it is successful, where it is found to have been granted on the basis of insufficient enquiries by the applicant, then the costs may subsequently be disallowed;
– that if the applicant is publicly funded, then prior authority from the Legal Services Commission may not readily be granted.

If an *Anton Piller* order is made against a client, it is essential to seek urgent and experienced advice, and within reason, bearing in mind the risk of committal, seek to delay until that advice is forthcoming. Keep a careful eye on the behaviour of those executing the order, for all of the reasons identified above.

3.72 Finally, note in particular the case of *Burgess v Burgess* [1996] 2 FLR 34, where at first instance before Hale J, the judge took the view that the application for an *Anton Piller* order had been made oppressively and without foundation and ordered the husband to pay the wife's costs of the order on an indemnity basis. In the Court of Appeal, the husband contended that criticisms made of him by the judge regarding the *Anton Piller* proceedings had been ill-founded and did not justify an indemnity costs order, especially since Douglas Brown J had properly granted the order on the ex parte application.

3.73 Waite LJ ([1996] 2 FLR 34, at 41) concluded as follows:

> 'Hale J was fully entitled to take note of the total lack of any evidence at the final hearing to support the charges of concealment or suppression of documents (and also of the late abandonment of the allegations on which their evidence was founded) and to draw the inference that the *Anton Piller* application had been made without justification. Costs were in her discretion, and she had every reason for ordering them to be paid on an indemnity basis. If she intended to sound a note of warning to others as to the consequences of making an ill-judged resort to *Anton Piller* relief in family proceedings – where it remains a rare weapon for use only in extreme or exceptional cases – she had good reason, in my view, for doing so.'

The message from this judgment could scarcely be clearer.

A case study

3.74 Whilst bearing in mind the warning in *Burgess* concerning *Anton Piller* orders, the ultimate success of the wife in *W v W (Periodical Payments: Pensions)* [1996] 2 FLR 480 rewards study. She embarked upon a long and determined struggle against a very unco-operative husband, during which process a series of judges made orders for committal (never ultimately implemented), granted applications for *Mareva* injunctions, for *subpoenas duces tecum* against the National Westminster Bank, and for an order that two companies connected with the husband's business be joined as respondents to the application for ancillary relief, principally to require them to provide discovery.

3.75   The case eventually came before Connell J, and the report sets out in some detail the trail followed by the wife, and her advisers, including her accountants (Messrs Coopers & Lybrand) in their determined pursuit of documents, and information about the whereabouts of the husband's wealth amid his maze of companies. Ultimately, Connell J took the husband's conduct of the case into account and penalised him as to costs; he then made an order, in part conventional, but in part less so, choosing to take the view that the court could vary a managed Equitable Life pension scheme as a post-nuptial settlement, and could nominate the wife as a dependant for all purposes, during her lifetime or until her re-marriage. He then ordered an amount of maintenance which was the subject of an attachment of earnings order (unopposed) against Equitable Life.

INTERCEPTION OF DOCUMENTS AND NON-DISCLOSURE: SOME HELPFUL GUIDANCE

3.76   Most practitioners will have encountered the situation where their client has expressed a willingness and/or an ability to 'acquire' (or has already 'acquired') some of the documentation relating to their spouse's finances, generally without their knowledge or consent. It may be that correspondence is still being sent to the address from which one spouse has departed, and has 'inadvertently' been opened; it may be that a briefcase or a study desk is left carelessly unlocked; or the actions in question may be rather more calculated and extreme. It has always been a difficult area for practitioners to advise on, and it is dealt with at some length in the SFLA *Good Practice in Family Law on Disclosure* mentioned in para **3.4** above. Aspects of this issue were dealt with in the case of *Hildebrand* (see paras **3.30** and **3.31** above), in 1992 by Waite J; some helpful guidelines have also now been laid down by Wilson J in *T v T (Interception of Documents)* [1994] 2 FLR 1083.

3.77   In that case, the wife was making an application for financial provision from her husband, following the breakdown of the marriage, and she undertook a number of activities to obtain information about his financial position, which are listed by the judge in some detail in his judgment.

In summary, she secretly photocopied financial documents kept by the husband at home, used force by breaking into his office, scoured the dustbin, opened letters addressed to him, misappropriated letters addressed to him, broke a window, entered his office and took his diary, and repeated this exercise a month or so later while he was there, on which occasion she snatched the diary and ran off with it.

3.78   The wife was also criticised for disclosing documents on a piecemeal basis through her solicitors. The judge called the timing of her production of some of the documents 'unacceptable'; original and copy documents which she had taken were discoverable and all those that she had in her possession at the discovery stage should have been disclosed at that time, that is at the time of the delivery of her questionnaire or earlier upon request. Instead, she suppressed some of the documents she had acquired for many months, producing one or two of them piecemeal and then 'a substantial number like a rabbit from a hat, just prior to the hearing'.

3.79   At a late stage in the proceedings the husband (although he had secretly opened some of her letters in the past) finally retaliated openly; he broke down the door of the room in which the wife kept her papers, removed a mass of them including numerous privileged documents, read them all and sent copies of some to his lawyers, who forthwith and without reading them, forwarded them to the wife's solicitors. On their advice, he also returned all the original documents to the wife.

3.80   The judge dealt first with whether or not the extent of the wife's activities was reprehensible. He observed that the husband had not made a full and frank presentation to the court of his financial resources, and that some of the documents that were taken by the wife had enabled the position to become clearer. She had anticipated, and it seems reasonably so, at the outset of the litigation that her husband would seek to reduce the level of her claim by understating his resources, and indeed he did. In the circumstances, the judge concluded that it was reasonable for her to take photocopies of such documents as she could locate without the use of force, and for that matter to scour the dustbin! However, she had gone far beyond that, and her timing of disclosure was unacceptable.

3.81   So did this amount to relevant conduct on her part in such a way as to affect the outcome of her application?

Wilson J agreed with Thorpe J in *P v P (Financial Relief: Non-Disclosure)* [1994] 2 FLR 381, that dishonest disclosure will more appropriately be reflected in the inference that the resources are larger than had been disclosed, which would then fall for consideration under the Matrimonial Causes Act 1973, s 25(2)(a), and/or in the order for costs. In *T v T*, Wilson J rejected the submission that the wife's actions amounted to conduct which should affect her substantive reward, but he held that they should have some relevance upon the issue of costs, although the precise extent of that would depend upon such other related factors as the husband's non-disclosure. He concluded by saying:

> 'Although the wife's activities may not have caused a significant increase in the costs, the court's discretion is wide enough to permit their inclusion in its survey of the litigation.'

Is non-disclosure financial misconduct – what are the risks?

3.82   Other more conventional situations which arise in relation to non-disclosure include that in the case of *P v P* mentioned above, in which Thorpe J held as a general proposition that a flagrant breach of the obligation to make full disclosure constituted financial conduct which could be brought into the balancing exercise to be carried out by the judge. This is the same point which was considered by Wilson J in *T v T*.

3.83   The case of *Frary v Frary and Another* [1993] 2 FLR 696, heard ultimately by the Court of Appeal, and also referred to above at para **3.42**, dealt primarily with the powers of the court on a production appointment, but there are some broad and helpful comments by Ralph Gibson LJ about the general approach to disclosure of documents, especially where third parties are involved, and the balance which needs to be achieved. He commented:

> 'As the decision of Balcombe J in *W v W* (1981) FLR 291 demonstrates, when a case is made that the respondent's assets have not been fully or properly described, a non party may be required to provide relevant information even if in doing so that person's private documents must be disclosed. All there is in this case, in my judgment, is the fact that Mrs R has "very, very considerable resources indeed", as the judge said, and as, I think, was plain from the evidence and general circumstances. Again, as Balcombe J indicated in *W v W* at p 293, if the respondent chooses not to arrange for Mrs R to provide information as to the precise limits of her means or cannot persuade her to do so, the remedy of the petitioner is to comment that Mrs R clearly has the ability, for example, to increase her contribution to the cost of the shared property if she is minded so to do. In the circumstances of this case I can see no sufficient relevance in the precise limits of Mrs R's very considerable resources to justify the order. The task of the court in the exercise of its discretion is to balance the interests of the petitioner in obtaining the information against the interests and the wishes of the third party not to divulge it – see *Morgan* [*v Morgan* [1977] 2 All ER 515].'

In *Frary* the costs were awarded in favour of the third party Mrs R, who had incurred the expense of representation at the production appointment, on an indemnity basis; a warning to all practitioners to be cautious in this particular field.

3.84   In summary, disclosure should be full and frank, not delivered piecemeal, not obtained by breaking and entering and not withheld without very good justification. The decision to withhold disclosure of evidence at an appropriate moment, perhaps for possible forensic benefits which may derive from presenting it with a flourish at a late stage, must be considered very cautiously and carefully with counsel. The guidelines on interception laid down by Wilson J in *T v T* are helpful, but it is interesting to note that, in that case, he to some extent forgave the wife's actions because she had genuine and, as it turned out, valid suspicions about her husband's lack of frank disclosure. A party without such justifiable suspicions will not be so freely able to scour dustbins and break into offices without facing stronger judicial reaction.

COSTS ORDERS ON DISCLOSURE

3.85   As the above cases demonstrate very clearly, the issue of costs and the consequence of mishandled disclosure, even in the more conventional situations, is one which practitioners must bear fully in mind. *H v H (Clean Break: Non-Disclosure: Costs)* [1994] 2 FLR 309 effectively illustrates the problem.

In this case, both parties wanted a financial clean break; the wife alleged that the husband had substantial hidden assets, probably in Switzerland, and the husband showed himself to be untruthful about his financial disclosure, though eventually making full disclosure. The decision on costs was influenced partly by the inadequacy of the husband's open offer, and the fact that his *Calderbank* offer was not in excess of the order finally made. However, in addition to that, Rodger Hayward Smith QC concluded that 'a substantial burden of costs has been occasioned by the husband's conduct of this litigation. He has, in the large measure, brought such a searching enquiry upon himself'.

3.86   The judge was accordingly asked by the wife's counsel to make a full indemnity order against the husband. He ultimately declined to do so, stating as follows:

> 'Having considered the arguments on both sides, it does seem to me that to make a full indemnity order against the husband is a Draconian thing to do.
>   I bear very much in mind his lack of disclosure and I have criticised him in my judgment. But it seems to me that justice can be done by making a standard order in favour of the wife. I am not persuaded that I should go as far as to make a Draconian indemnity costs order that is asked for. I decline to make such an order.'

However, in the *Burgess* case (referred to in para **3.72** above), the Court of Appeal upheld an order by Hale J, ordering the husband to pay the wife's costs on an indemnity basis for an oppressive and unfounded *Anton Piller* application.

ORDERS FOR WASTED COSTS

3.87   A few months after the hearing of *H v H*, Ewbank J dealt with the case of *C v C (Wasted Costs Order)* [1994] 2 FLR 34. The case is an extreme example, but is worth study. The lump sum award to the wife was £20,000; the costs of the case amounted to £130,000 and in the later stages those of the wife were funded by the Legal Aid Board (now the Legal Services Commission).

3.88   The husband made an application under s 51 of the Supreme Court Act 1981 (which provides for payment of costs wasted by a legal representative's improper, unreasonable or negligent acts or omissions) for his costs to be paid by the wife's solicitor. The wife in turn made a claim against her solicitor, asking for repayment of costs already paid and for unpaid legal aid costs to be disallowed. The wife's solicitors joined the wife's first counsel in the action. The

Legal Aid Board claimed against the wife's solicitors asking for the wife's legal aid costs to be disallowed. The husband claimed against the Legal Aid Board for the balance of his costs and he made a claim against his wife for costs also.

3.89   The test previously required under s 51 of the 1981 Act had always been a high one 'of a serious dereliction of duty'. At the close of a 14-day hearing, Ewbank J held that there was no suggestion of improper conduct, but he found quite clearly that there had been a massive waste of costs, incurred as a result of the unreasonableness of solicitor and counsel. In his judgment, he recited the history of the case in considerable detail, referring to the correspondence between solicitors, the terms of the proposals which were put forward, the nature of the disclosure which was made and the relationships between the parties, and set out the case put forward to the district judge at the original hearing. He concluded by making a very detailed order covering a period during which the case was conducted from August 1990 to August 1992, and dealing with (breaking down into precise percentages) the various claims by the husband, the wife, the wife's solicitors and the Legal Aid Board.

3.90   In his judgment, he drew attention to the case of *Ridehalgh v Horsefield, and Watson v Watson (Wasted Costs Orders)* [1994] 2 FLR 194, which the Court of Appeal had decided whilst the case was in progress, and in which it had laid down guidelines in relation to wasted costs applications in dealing with a collection of six cases. That judgment revolved around the construction of the words in s 51(7) of the Supreme Court Act 1981. There were representations for an adjournment until the Court of Appeal judgment had been delivered, but Ewbank J decided the case should proceed, with counsel being given the opportunity of making further submissions based upon that judgment.

3.91   Without embarking here on a very detailed discussion on wasted costs, it is important to emphasise that any practitioner who may have concerns about the conduct of a case on either side, and the resulting costs implications, should certainly review the current case-law carefully. If it is possible to demonstrate a clear link between improper, unreasonable or negligent conduct (a phrase which will be rigorously interpreted) and wasted costs, then there may be some justification for an application. Bear in mind, however, that threats to apply for wasted costs orders should not be used lightly nor to intimidate the opposition, and applications are generally best left until after the trial.

3.92   When considering applying for an order, points to be weighed are whether it is a clear case; whether there is a reasonable explanation for what has happened; what costs can be shown as wasted by the conduct complained of; what are the economics of the litigation; and whether this is the right time to be contemplating an application. It should not be approached lightly.

3.93   To avoid the risks of such orders, practitioners must take care to analyse information accurately, review cases (and merits) regularly, keep full records of interviews, telephone calls and conferences, and to maintain the balance already discussed, between the obligations of full investigation and disclosure, and the risk of incurring unnecessary costs. If an application is made against the client, contact the Solicitors Indemnity Fund; and bear in mind that there may be a conflict of interest with the client. Counsel are also vulnerable, and they too must review cases afresh when they receive the papers again, which they are not always asked to do. The need for commitment of solicitors and counsel to a practical and a financially sensible approach is increasingly apparent – not unreasonably, perhaps both the client and the court would say.

Chapter 4

UNDERSTANDING BUSINESS ACCOUNTS

INTRODUCTION

4.1 As mentioned in Chapter 2 above, in cases of financial complexity where there are substantial assets, an accountant will normally be employed as adviser on financial matters and, prospectively, as expert witness. The interpretation of the business accounts, and the identification of the matters to be followed up by questionnaire or other investigation, will then fall to the accountant. It is, however, usual and useful for the solicitor to have a general knowledge of the interpretation of accounts.

4.2 The annual financial statements of all but small companies, as defined at **4.29**, will comprise a balance sheet, a profit and loss account, a cash flow statement, a directors' report and supporting explanatory notes. If the company has subsidiaries, it must also produce a consolidated balance sheet (as well as the company's own balance sheet) and a consolidated profit and loss account (in place of the company's own profit and loss account). Examples of these statements for a fictitious company, Favourite Fashions Limited, are included in the Appendix and extracts from them are reviewed in this chapter.

The balance sheet

4.3 It is important to recognise that the balance sheet (or consolidated balance sheet) of a company or group is no more than a financial 'snapshot' at the date to which it is made up. It is a summary of the assets and liabilities, the net amount of which is equal to the capital employed in the business.

The profit and loss account

4.4 The profit and loss account of a business shows the sources of income earned and categories of expense incurred during the period ending on the balance sheet date, the difference between total income and total expenditure being the profit or loss for that period.

The cash flow statement

4.5 The cash flow statement shows how the expenditure charged in the profit and loss account is linked to the movements between the opening and closing balance sheets, and how the results of the company's operations for the year and its investment or disinvestment activities affect the inward and outward flow of cash. A review of these statements over a period of years may provide useful additional information about the ability of the company to generate cash, some of which may possibly be made available for the purposes of achieving a financial settlement.

Notes to the accounts

4.6 Much of the information required by company law to be presented with the annual report to shareholders is contained in the notes to the accounts. These supplement and amplify the items contained in the balance sheet and profit and loss account. They include such matters as:

(a) details of the accounting policies adopted in compiling the accounts;
(b) more detailed information regarding the changes in fixed assets and the composition of the current assets and liabilities;
(c) details of the subsidiary and associated companies;
(d) particulars of the movements in reserves.

The directors' report

4.7 Company law requires limited companies to present a directors' report as part of the annual financial reporting to shareholders. This contains supplementary information, on prescribed matters, including:

(a) a description of the principal activities of the company or group;
(b) particulars of any significant differences between the book values and the market values of fixed assets;
(c) details of directors' interests in the share capital of the company, including options;
(d) details of dividends paid and proposed.

THE BALANCE SHEET

4.8 Figure 1 shows the balance sheet of Famous Fashions Limited at 31 March 2001.

Figure 1: Balance sheet at 31 March 2001

	Note	2001 £		2000 £	
Fixed Assets					
Tangible assets	8	830,224		714,426	
Current Assets					
Stocks and work in progress	9	829,201		986,432	
Debtors	10	1,006,612		1,025,719	
Cash at bank and in hand		482,103		263,459	
		2,317,916		2,275,610	
Creditors:					
Amounts falling due within one year	11	(1,124,200)		(1,245,930)	
Provisions for liabilities and charges	12	(125,556)		(48,712)	
Net current assets			1,068,160		980,968
Total Assets less Current Liabilities			1,898,384		1,695,394
Creditors:					
Amounts falling due after more than one year	13		(250,000)		(250,000)
			1,648,384		1,445,394
Share Capital and Reserves					
Called up share capital	14		5,000		5,000
Profit and loss account			1,643,384		1,440,394
Equity shareholders' funds			1,648,384		1,445,394

The balance sheet is not necessarily a statement of the value of the assets and liabilities but simply a summary of the amounts at which they are carried in the books. It is simplistic to assume that the value of a company is equal to the net assets or capital employed shown in its balance sheet.

Fixed assets

4.9   Fixed assets, such as land and buildings, plant and machinery, equipment and motor vehicles, are normally recorded in the books at cost. If the nature of the asset is such that it depreciates over time, a charge for such depreciation will be made in the accounts each year and the accumulated depreciation will be deducted from the cost in arriving at the value shown in the balance sheet.

4.10   Some companies revalue certain of their fixed assets from time to time, notably freehold and long leasehold property, and then apply depreciation to the revalued amounts in their books. In the absence of such revaluations, the book value of land and buildings may be quite different from their saleable value in the property market. Whether this is a matter that needs to be pursued is considered further in Chapter 5, 'Valuing the Business'.

4.11   The accounts and the notes to them should provide sufficient detail to identify the main categories of fixed asset and the amount of the company's investment in each category after deducting accumulated depreciation. The amount shown in the balance sheet will normally be the subject of an explanatory note such as shown in Figure 2.

Figure 2: Explanatory note as to fixed assets

Group	Freehold property £	Plant, machinery and vehicles £	Fixtures and fittings £	Total £
Cost or valuation				
At 1 April 2000	350,000	435,600	396,420	1,182,020
Additions	–	60,000	160,700	220,700
Disposals	–	(15,500)	–	(15,500)
	350,000	480,100	557,120	1,387,220
Depreciation				
At 1 April 2000	28,000	249,600	189,994	467,594
Provided during the year	3,500	43,760	42,142	89,402
At 31 March 2001	31,500	293,360	232,136	556,996
Net book value				
At 1 April 2000	322,000	186,000	206,426	714,426
At 31 March 2001	318,500	186,740	324,984	830,224

Current assets

4.12   Current assets typically include stock in trade, work in progress, trade debts receivable, other amounts receivable, cash and bank balances.

Stock and work in progress

4.13   Stock and work in progress are required to be shown in the accounts at the lower of cost and net realisable value. If the information is not given in the accounts or notes, the amount of the provisions deducted in arriving at the balance sheet figure should be ascertained. If there is any likelihood that the results of the business have been manipulated in order to present a less attractive picture than the true one, the inclusion of unnecessarily high provisions against stock and work in progress is one of the more obvious possibilities. This would have the effect both of reducing the book value of the net assets and of reducing the profits against which the unnecessary provisions have been charged. In the typical case where a run of accounts for several years is obtained, it will be possible to see how the provisions relate each year to the gross book value of stock and work in progress and this may indicate whether provisions have been significantly increased since the breakdown of the marriage.

4.14   It can be seen from the balance sheet in Figure 1 that there has been a considerable decrease in the level of stocks compared to the previous year. More information can be derived from the balance sheet notes. The relevant stock note is set out in Figure 3. The note shows that the decrease in the value of stocks at the year end is primarily due to the lower level of finished goods. This should alert those examining the accounts to the possibility of a high level of provisions against finished goods at the year end.

Figure 3: Stock note

Stocks	2001	2000
	£	£
Work in progress	523,160	562,204
Finished goods and goods for resale	306,041	424,228
	829,201	986,432

Trade debtors and other receivables

4.15   Trade debtors and other receivables are also included after making provision for bad and doubtful debts. Similar information about the level of such provisions and the way they have varied over recent years should be reviewed in order to see whether there is any indication of unnecessarily high provisions being included to reduce the perceived profitability of the company and the net asset value appearing in the balance sheet.

4.16   The balance sheet shows a small reduction in debtors during the year, and on a first reading would not indicate any deliberate attempt to reduce net asset values. However, the related notes should be reviewed to obtain a more detailed picture: see Figure 4.

Figure 4: Note as to debtors

Debtors: amounts falling due within one year	2001	2000
	£	£
Trade debtors	942,581	1,007,028
Prepayments and other amounts receivable	64,031	18,691
	1,006,612	1,025,719

4.17   Other amounts receivable may include money due from one or both of the parties to the company. While loans to directors of more than £5,000 are illegal, it is common for the controlling shareholders of family companies to run a current account with the company which may pay bills on their behalf. Such expenditure may include personal expenditure incurred on credit cards. Such accounts are referred to in the Companies Act 1985 as 'quasi-loans' and, in private companies, are not prohibited. Any combination of loans, quasi-loans and credit transactions between a company and a director, if in excess of £5,000, is required to be disclosed in the audited accounts. However, it is not uncommon in the accounts of family companies to find that the provisions of the Companies Act 1985 have not been observed in this respect, and such balances may have been included under other receivables.

Cash and bank balances

4.18   The level of cash and bank balances is important as an indication of the liquid position of the company. If there are substantial liquid funds, it will be appropriate to consider whether, and if so to what extent, they can be made available to the parties for the purposes of a financial settlement. The level of bank balances at the balance sheet date can quite easily be affected by the actions of the management of the company. If they wish to reduce apparent liquidity they can do so, for example, by paying creditors earlier than necessary or by building up stock levels. If there has been a significant reduction in liquidity in the latest balance sheet, enquiries should be made to see whether any such manipulation may have taken place. This might include asking for details of the level of bank balances shown by the management accounts from time to time during the previous year.

Current liabilities

4.19   Current liabilities include creditors and accounts payable within one year, and bank borrowings or overdrafts. Reference has been made above to the possibility that the amount due to trade creditors may have been reduced by early payment in order to reduce the apparent liquidity of the company, and to the need to review the fluctuations in the level of bank balances. Such a review should also cover the fluctuations in the level of creditors, if there is any reason to suspect that this may have taken place.

Creditors

4.20   An analysis of the accounts payable, other than trade creditors, should be obtained. Any amount included under such a heading which is due by the company to one of the parties should be included among the personal assets of that party. The creditor note in the notes to the accounts will provide detail on whether the company owes money to one of the parties: see Figure 5. In the example given, it can be seen that the directors' current account has increased by almost one-third compared to the previous year.

Figure 5: Notes as to creditors

Creditors: falling due within one year	2001	2000
	£	£
Director's current account	53,000	40,000
Tax and social security	149,218	261,968
Trade creditors	902,612	923,014
Accruals and deferred income	4,370	5,948
Proposed dividend	15,000	15,000
	1,124,200	1,245,930

Provisions

4.21 The level of provisions for liabilities and charges may indicate an attempt at deliberate manipulation of the accounts. Any large increase in provisions on the face of the balance sheet should suggest that further investigation is necessary: see Figure 6. The note clearly shows that the increase in the total is due to an £80,000 increase in the advertising provision. This provision will reduce the net asset position of the company and the profit figure for the year.

Figure 6: Notes as to provision for liabilities and charges

Provisions for Liabilities and Charges	Balance at 1.4.00	Movement in year	Balance at 31.3.01
	£	£	£
Advertising	5,000	80,000	85,000
Repairs and Maintenance	43,712	(3,156)	40,556
	48,712	76,844	125,556

Bank and other borrowings

4.22 The level of bank and other borrowings is an important element in the consideration of the company's liquid position, and whether it is reasonable to expect money to be made available from the company in order to meet the financial requirements of the parties. Where there are substantial borrowings, information should therefore be sought as to the terms of repayment agreed with the bank or other lender. It may also be valuable to seek copies of information provided to the lenders regarding the plans and prospects of the company in order to ensure that that information is consistent with the picture which is being portrayed in the context of the matrimonial proceedings. In the typical situation where the husband is the controlling shareholder of a family company with substantial borrowings, he may be tempted to show a more pessimistic view of the future to his divorcing wife than to his bank manager, who wants to be reassured about the security for the loan.

Share capital and reserves

4.23   The net assets, arrived at by deducting the total liabilities from the total assets, are equal to the total of the invested capital and reserves of the company, which would be shown on the face of the balance sheet, supported if necessary by detailed analysis in the notes to the accounts. The extent of the ownership of the parties will be determined by the proportion of each class of capital that they hold and by the rights attaching to each such class. The Memorandum and Articles of Association of the company should therefore be reviewed to establish the rights attaching to each class of share capital, if there is more than one such class. It should, however, be borne in mind that the holders of 75 per cent of the voting share capital may be able to change the Memorandum and Articles of Association, subject always to the obligation not to oppress minority shareholders.

4.24   The movements in the company's reserves over the period covered by the accounts should be reviewed to see whether any abnormal amounts have been taken directly to reserves, rather than being passed through the profit and loss account. This is now less common than it used to be but, for example, surpluses arising on a revaluation of fixed assets can still be taken direct to reserves.

PROFIT AND LOSS ACCOUNT

4.25   For a limited company, the contents of the profit and loss account are prescribed by the Companies Act 1985. Although it is not required to be published, all companies must also produce a detailed trading and profit and loss account setting out their income and expenditure in more detail than are required in the published accounts: see Figure 7. Copies of these detailed accounts, which have to be produced in order to enable the company to settle its tax liabilities with the Inland Revenue, should also be obtained and are likely to be a fruitful source of additional information to that given in the published profit and loss account. It is important to ensure that the two documents arrive at the same profit figure.

Figure 7: Detailed trading profit and loss account for the year ended 31 March 2001

	2001		2000	
	£	£	£	£
Turnover		6,963,245		6,843,920
Less: cost of sales				
Opening stock	986,432		855,000	
Purchases	4,593,519		4,554,453	
Manufacturing wages/NI	1,014,981		976,603	
Depreciation	44,701		69,000	
Less: closing stock	(829,201)		(986,432)	
		(5,810,432)		(5,468,624)
Gross profit		1,152,813		1,126,656
Less: Distribution costs				
Carriage in	30,745		40,229	
Depreciation	22,351		34,500	
Petrol and diesel	43,850		41,725	
Distribution wages/NI	162,214		145,158	
		(259,160)		(261,612)
Less: Administrative costs				
Entertaining	34,533		12,320	
Administrative salaries/NI	90,553		86,289	
Rates	18,514		15,232	
Light and heat	5,129		4,390	
Bad debts	3,598		2,560	
Directors' salaries	160,000		149,000	
National insurance	14,050		14,020	
Directors' pensions	15,000		31,000	
Depreciation	22,350		34,500	
Telephone and stationery	7,046		6,387	
Repairs and renewals	1,196		1,163	
Auditors' remuneration	19,000		18,000	
Travel and advertising	82,423		22,203	
Sundry	28,528		18,630	
		(501,920)		(415,694)
		391,733		697,990

While the balance sheet is a snapshot of the financial position at a particular date, the profit and loss account covers the total result of the company's trading activities over the period, typically one year.

REVIEW OF FLUCTUATIONS

4.26 Unusual features are often best identified by a comparison of the profit and loss accounts for several years, to see whether there have been significant changes in the relationship of key figures to one another. In many businesses the relationship between gross profit and sales will be reasonably constant from one year to another. (The gross profit is the amount arrived at by deducting the cost of sales from the value of sales or turnover; in a trading company the cost of sales comprises the value of opening stock plus purchases, less the value of closing stock; in a manufacturing company production costs such as raw materials, factory wages and overheads will come into the calculation of cost of sales.) If there has been a significant reduction in the level of gross profit, it may indicate that there has been an increase in the level of provisions made against stock and work in progress. Such an increase in provisions may of course be made for entirely legitimate reasons, but there is also the possibility that profits could have been deliberately reduced in this way.

4.27 Similarly, the details of the expenditure on the expense categories making up overhead and selling expenses should be reviewed for unusual fluctuations. A substantial increase in advertising expenditure or repairs and maintenance may, for example, indicate that expenditure which would otherwise have been incurred in future years has been accelerated, possibly with a view to depressing the results in the short term, but to the benefit of the profitability of subsequent years. If there is very substantial expenditure on travelling and entertaining in a family-controlled company, it may be of interest to enquire as to the extent to which such expenditure has been incurred by or on behalf of the parties. Sometimes such expenditure includes matters which are not strictly expenditure of the company, which should therefore be added back in considering the level of the company's profitability.

The level and trend of profits before tax is normally the most important single factor in estimating the value of the business. This is referred to in more detail in Chapter 5, 'Valuing the Business'.

THE LEVEL OF TAX CHARGE

4.28 The review of the accounts should include a comparison of the level of the annual tax charge with the profits before tax to see whether the rate of tax appears reasonable by reference to the standard rate of corporation tax. If the tax charge is higher than the standard rate, it is an indication that expenditure charged in the profit and loss account has been disallowed in arriving at the taxable profit of the company. This may be for entirely normal and legitimate reasons; for example the amortisation of leasehold property is not an allowable deduction for tax purposes and if such an amortisation charge is substantial, it may distort the relationship between the profit before tax and the tax charge.

However, it is also possible that a high level of tax indicates that substantial personal expenditure on such matters as travel and entertaining may have been absorbed by the company, and this should be identified both for the purposes of forming a proper view of the true profitability of the company, and also because it is important in relation to the standard of living of the parties and the benefits obtained from the company.

SMALL COMPANIES

4.29 Small companies are permitted to file abbreviated financial statements which do not require a directors' report, profit and loss account, statement of recognised gains and losses or many of the notes and are exempt from some of the more onerous accounting standards and disclosure requirements. Nevertheless, the detailed trading and profit and loss account referred to in **4.25** will still have to be produced for tax purposes and should usually be called for.

4.30 A company is small if, in two of the last three years or in its first year, two out of the three following conditions are met:

Annual turnover	Does not exceed £2,800,000
Total gross assets	Does not exceed £1,400,000
Average number of employees	Does not exceed 50

4.31 Companies with turnover of not more than £350,000 and total gross assets of not more than £1,400,000 (and which are not part of a group whose aggregate turnover and total gross assets exceed these limits) are also exempt from the normal requirement to have their financial statements audited.

PARTNERSHIPS AND SOLE TRADERS

4.32 The accounts of partnerships and sole traders are not prescribed by statute but have to be produced in order to enable the taxation liabilities of the business to be established. If there is a partnership agreement, it may contain provisions relating to the partnership accounts and, if these include a requirement that the accounts show a true and fair view, will be required to comply with the Statements of Standard Accounting Policies laid down by the accountancy profession from time to time. Otherwise, the detailed trading and profit and loss account is likely to be similar to that produced by a limited company. The balance sheet will typically be less detailed than that produced by a company and less detail will be given in the notes to the accounts. There is no requirement for a cash flow statement or for a directors' report to be produced when drawing up the accounts of partnerships or sole traders.

4.33 In place of the share capital and reserves of a limited company, the accounts of unincorporated businesses will have the proprietors' capital and undrawn profits. In a partnership, copies should be sought of the detailed movements on the partners' capital and current accounts for at least the same period as that covered by the accounts produced.

Chapter 5

VALUING THE BUSINESS

LISTED COMPANIES

5.1   The valuation approach described in this chapter is relevant to all forms of business entity for which an existing market price does not already exist. In the event that the main business to be considered is a listed company in which the family hold a minority shareholding, those shares will normally be valued by reference to the listed market price. However, the disposal of a substantial block of shares in a listed company may not be achievable at the currently quoted price and it may be necessary to deduct a discount to allow for the size of the block of shares. It is unusual for such a discount to exceed 10 per cent.

5.2   Directors of listed companies sometimes contend that they could not sell shares in the company without causing a loss of confidence in the company on the part of the stock market and shareholders. In fact, shares can normally be disposed of in these circumstances without such results, as can be demonstrated by reference to actual sales in the past. Provided that care is taken to ensure that the right messages are conveyed to the market, the sale will not be seen as a signal that the director has lost confidence in the company. Typically, a placing of the shares will be arranged by the company's brokers with one or more financial institutions at a price marginally below the market price. Exceptionally, if the shares are already out of favour with the market and sellers in the market outweigh buyers, such a placing may be difficult and a larger discount may have to be contemplated.

5.3   On rare occasions, the family may hold a controlling interest in a listed company, in which case the normal approach would be to start from the listed price of the company's shares, and then to add a premium to reflect the fact that the shareholding is a controlling interest. This will certainly be relevant if the parties and their children and trusts settled by the parties together hold the controlling interest. If a controlling interest was reached only by including other, more remote, members of the family, then it is more likely that the simple approach of using the listed share price would be adopted.

UNLISTED COMPANIES

Introduction

5.4   Although reference has been made earlier (see Chapter 2, para **2.21**) to the judicial warnings against wasting costs on expensive and unnecessary valuations of family businesses, it is often necessary to form at least a general idea of the value of such a business where it has any significance to the assessment of the financial resources of the parties.

5.5   An exceptional case, in which there would probably be little point in trying to attribute value to a business, is where the profits are no more than the net income of the party carrying on the business, and therefore the value is no more than the capitalised value of that party's earning capacity. This appears to have been the position in *B v B (Financial Provision)* [1989] 1 FLR 119, where the husband was a practising architect and substantial costs seem to have been incurred arguing about the value of his architect's practice.

5.6   Following Booth J in *Evans*, the desirable attributes of a valuation therefore appear to be that it should be a broad assessment, that it should not be expensive or meaningless, and that it should not seek to achieve precision. The approach described in this chapter seeks to follow these guidelines, recognising that the amount of detail into which it may be appropriate to go will be influenced by the likelihood that the shares in question will in fact be sold.

5.7   Where the company has grown well beyond the stage where it is no more than the '*alter ego*' of the controlling shareholder, but has a substantial separable value that would survive in the event of his or her departure from the company, an estimate of the value of the business is necessary to a proper understanding of the total financial resources of the parties. At the very least, if the interest in the family company is to be retained by the husband, its value may have significance in determining how much of the other assets should be made available to the wife. If, for example, there is a substantial family business worth, say, £8 million and there are liquid assets outside the company of £1 million, the wife is likely to be entitled to a larger share of the £1 million liquid assets than she would be if the business did not exist or was not to be retained by the husband.

5.8   Exceptionally, there may be a real possibility that shares in the company will be sold. This may arise particularly where the husband is approaching retirement age and there is no expectation that the next generation of the family will succeed him in the business. Occasionally, it is the declared intention of the husband to seek to dispose of the business, or it is one which has been the subject of previous takeover interest from other companies. It is also possible that the wife is a substantial shareholder in the business and that one way of extracting liquid resources from the company may be for the company to purchase the wife's shares. In such a case, the value at which a purchase is to be made will have important tax consequences and will need to be considered with some care.

5.9   Following the decision in *White v White*, to which reference has been made in Chapter 1, the value of family companies is likely to assume more importance in order to enable the court to apply the yardstick of equality. It remains to be seen whether the presumption that the family business will not be sold to generate the funds needed to meet the wife's claims can still be relied upon.

5.10 In approaching the exercise of making the required assessment of value, we first need to define what we mean by 'value'. The usual approach is to consider the price which might reasonably be expected to be achieved in a sale on the open market between a willing seller and a willing buyer on the basis that both parties have equal knowledge, and that each is acting for self-interest and for gain. In making such an estimate, precision is impossible and a broad assessment is normally all that can reasonably be expected. In practice, negotiations would take place between the prospective purchaser and seller, in which each would have in mind a range of values within which he might conclude a deal. If the top end of the purchaser's range is not higher than the bottom end of the seller's range, no deal will be concluded, but if the two ranges overlap the price arrived at might lie anywhere in the area of overlap, depending upon the negotiating skill of the parties. There is therefore a range of reasonable values within which the result might lie, rather than any one 'right' figure.

5.11 In approaching the estimation of value, it is important to appreciate that all value lies in the future and that the valuation is the amount that a purchaser would pay for the future benefits of ownership of the asset that he is buying. Where that asset is a shareholding in a company, the rights of future ownership will be defined by the Memorandum and Articles of Association and are likely to depend considerably on the extent to which the shareholding carries control or influence over the company.

5.12 Since a purchaser will be influenced, in deciding how much he will pay for the shareholding, by the alternative investment opportunities open to him, valuations are usually made by comparison with the prices that might be paid for other similar investments, making adjustments for the points of difference. However the valuation is carried out, it can be no more than a matter of estimation and opinion, since only a real open market sale will establish the true value of the asset.

INFORMATION ABOUT THE COMPANY

5.13 At the outset of the valuation, the valuer will need to obtain a general understanding of the company covering such matters as:

(a)   the nature of its activities;
(b)   the quality and continuity of its management;
(c)   the operating conditions under which it carries on business;

(d)   the sensitivity of the business and exposure to risk; and

(e)   its future plans.

SOURCES OF INFORMATION

The accounts

5.14   The accounts for a period of at least three years will be one of the primary sources of information required for the purpose of the valuation. We have described in Chapter 4 the type of information that can be sought in reviewing the accounts of the company.

Asset valuation

5.15   If the market value of any of the assets of the company is significantly different from the amount at which it is included in the balance sheet, the difference in value may affect the value of the shares in the company. This would not apply to stock and work in progress, which is required to be included at the lower of cost and net realisable value.

5.16   The most likely type of asset to be stated in the accounts at a figure significantly different from its market value, would be freehold or long leasehold property. It is reasonable to enquire whether any recent valuations of such assets have been obtained, but it would not normally be appropriate to seek to make valuations specifically for the purposes of the family proceedings, unless it was clear that the results were going to be very significant in relation to both the valuation of the company's shares and the resolution of the financial arrangements between the parties.

Tax information

5.17   Copies of the company's tax returns and, more particularly, corporation tax computations, and of forms P11D completed in respect of the parties, will provide information about the extent to which expenditure has been incurred which is not allowable for tax, and which may therefore need to be adjusted in forming a proper view of the profitability of the company. This information may also be relevant to considerations of the standards of living and the benefits obtained by the parties from the company.

Access to the accountants

5.18   Wherever possible, the company's accountants should be given authority to speak to the accountants carrying out the valuation of the company's shares, with a view to the efficient transmission of relevant information. This is more easily achieved in cases where the whole of the capital of the company is within the hands of the immediate family. Where others have a significant interest in the company, considerations of confidentiality may arise – see further Chapter 3, para **3.46** above.

Access to the management

5.19   If it is possible for the valuing accountants to speak directly to the key members of the management of the company about its activities, operations and prospects, this can greatly facilitate the obtaining of the required information quickly and economically. The valuing accountant will need to take into account the possibility that the person providing the information may have an interest in presenting it in a way that might influence the valuation upwards or downwards, and that the information being provided may not be entirely objective.

Information provided to lenders

5.20   One way of balancing any information that may have been biased towards depressing the valuation, is to seek copies of information provided to banks or other providers of loan finance. Where a husband may tell his divorcing wife that the future is bleak, he is likely to paint a rosier picture to his bankers upon whose continuing support he depends. The valuer may sometimes conclude that the true position lies somewhere in the middle.

MAJOR INFLUENCES ON VALUE

The significance of the size of the shareholding

5.21   In considering how much a purchaser might pay to acquire the shareholding that is to be valued, it is necessary to consider what benefits will be obtained from its future ownership. Among the most important of the rights attaching to a shareholding is the extent to which it carries control over the company.

5.22   While for many purposes, particularly the calculation of tax liabilities, a narrow view is taken of the identity of the shareholder in deciding what asset has to be valued, it is common in the Family Division to take a broader view. Where, for example, shares are held by members of a family and there is no reason to doubt that they will co-operate together to their best mutual advantage, it is normal to look at the value of the family holding as a whole, and then to take the value of each party's holding as a proportional part of that total valuation.

Minority interests
5.23   Normally a minority shareholder in a company can only obtain benefit from the ownership of his shares by receiving a dividend, if one is declared by

the controlling shareholders, and ultimately by selling his shareholding at a profit, if he is able to do so. A minority shareholder will therefore be very concerned with the prospect of future dividends in the short term, and the possibility of future sale at a profit eventually. Frequently, the prospect of selling a minority shareholding in a private company is so remote that the prospective dividends are the main influence on the valuation of a minority shareholding.

Controlling interests
5.24   Different considerations arise where the shareholding carries control of the company. The holder of the controlling interest now has power over its earning capacity and can determine how its earnings are to be deployed; what dividends are to be paid; how much is to be paid by way of remuneration to the directors; and how much profit will be ploughed back into the company to build up its value in a way that will ultimately affect the capital gain that will arise if and when the company comes to be sold. Such a shareholder will normally be interested primarily in the prospective earnings of the company.

Asset values
5.25   The future benefit to the shareholders of the company's ownership of its assets is usually less directly relevant to the value of its shares than earnings and dividends. The exception to this would be where the purpose of the company is to hold assets, for example if it is a property holding company or an investment holding company. Very exceptionally, there may be a prospect that the company will be broken up and its assets realised, in which case the amount that can be realised will become significant.

The future
5.26   It is important to keep in mind that the valuation will be influenced primarily by future earnings, future dividends and the future benefit of the company's ownership of its assets, when considering the information available regarding the past. The purchaser of a shareholding is not buying an interest in the past, but in the future, and the information about the past is relevant only to the extent that it is helpful in forming a view about the future.

THE VALUATION PROCESS

The valuation basis

5.27   It is sometimes said that valuations are arrived at on an earnings basis, or on a dividend basis, or on an asset basis. It is, however, unusual for the purchaser of shares in a company to be influenced by only one of these three things. The reality is more likely to be that they will all influence the price that he is prepared to pay, but that the emphasis that he will place on each of these three factors will vary. For example, where the company is a normal trading company earning substantial profits and the shareholding to be valued is a controlling interest, the level of future earnings will carry the most weight in the mind of the purchaser, and his primary approach will be to establish the appropriate level of earnings and then to decide what multiplier to apply to it, to arrive at his value. However, the company's capacity to pay dividends will have an influence on that multiplier. If the profits generated are likely to be readily realisable through the company's ability to distribute substantial dividends (if the controlling shareholders so wish), the purchaser may be inclined to apply a higher multiple than he would if the earnings were likely to have to be locked into the company and ploughed back for a considerable period before any cash return on the investment could be expected.

5.28 Similarly, the extent of the asset backing for the price initially arrived at by reference to earnings, will have an influence on the extent of the risk involved in the investment, since high asset backing reduces the risk entailed in the investment. Conversely, investment in a company with very high earnings but very low assets may be regarded as carrying a higher risk and therefore this may reduce the multiplier to be applied to those earnings.

5.29 Where the shareholding to be valued is a minority shareholding, the prospective dividend is likely to be the main influence on value and the valuation exercise then requires the determination of the base level of dividend and of the return that the investor would require on his investment, in the form of a dividend yield. Once the prospective dividend and the dividend yield have been determined, calculation of value is a matter of simple arithmetic.

Property and investment companies

5.30 In one (more rarely met) category of valuation, the asset value is the most important factor in the mind of a prospective purchaser. This category would include investment and property holding companies, the value of which is determined primarily by the underlying asset value reduced normally by a discount. This is to take into account the fact that it is generally more attractive to hold an asset directly than through an intermediate holding company, particularly if the holder has less than 100 per cent ownership of the holding company. Allowance also has to be made for the tax that might be payable if the assets were in future to be distributed to the shareholders.

Break-up values

5.31 Asset value is also the primary factor in the valuation, for those companies where an eventual break-up and realisation of the underlying assets is the most likely way in which the purchaser would obtain any value from his investment. Such companies would include those which are making losses with no immediate prospect of a return to profitability. Break-up value may also be relevant to companies which are currently earning very low profits, where the valuation may reflect a balance between the value that may be reached if the company's future goes well and higher profit levels are established in the future, and the break-up value that may be all that can be obtained if this does not happen and the company's position deteriorates.

5.32 In considering break-up values, it is important to bear in mind that the values obtained may be significantly different from those shown in the company's balance sheet. While some assets such as properties may be included in the balance sheet at less than the value that could be obtained on a break-up, others are likely to realise substantially less. In particular, stock and work in progress of a company that is broken up will frequently realise only a fraction of its cost and a substantial allowance may have to be made for bad debts in considering the realisable value of trade debtors, since it is often very much more difficult to obtain payment from a customer who no longer depends upon the company for continuity of supply. The experience of insolvency practitioners shows that many such customers produce reasons for not paying the amounts shown to be due, which in the end have the effect of reducing amounts collectable.

5.33 In considering break-up value, allowance also has to be made for liabilities not included in the normal balance sheet, which is drawn up on the assumption that the company is a going concern. Such liabilities would include redundancy pay for those whose employment would be brought to an end, and damages for breach of contract in ending other contractual relationships between the company and those with whom it does business. The costs of realising assets and liquidating the company would also have to be allowed for and the purchaser would be inclined to make a prudent allowance for all these things in deciding what return might ultimately be achieved on a break-up. It is emphasised, however, that considerations of break-up value are the exception rather than the rule.

Selection of price/earnings ratio or dividend yield

In general
5.34 Returning to the more usual situation where the main influence on valuation is earnings or dividends, and assuming that the valuer has determined what level of earnings or dividend should form the basis for his valuation, it remains to consider what multiplier or price/earnings ratio or dividend yield should be applied to arrive at the value.

5.35 It is at this point relevant to consider the return that would be available to the purchaser on alternative investments. The more similar the alternative investment is to the one that has to be valued, the more relevant the comparison will be. In valuing a substantial business, comparison with shares in companies listed on the Stock Exchange is likely to be appropriate. The valuer will normally consider the price/earnings ratio and dividend yield currently obtainable on shares generally, as reflected in the FT-Actuaries Share Index, as an indicator of the general investment climate against which the valuation is being carried out. He is likely to consider most closely the figures for the particular sector of the index most closely relevant to the company that has to be valued.

5.36   In some cases, it may be possible from these general considerations to form a view on the corresponding return that might be required by an investor in the shares in the company which has to be valued but, even in the context of a broad approach, it will often be worthwhile to try to identify a small number of individual companies within the same industry, that have points of similarity with the subject company. A review should then be made of the financial information available about those companies, with a view to identifying the main features of difference between them and the subject company for which adjustment would need to be made.

Matters requiring adjustments

5.37   The most important matters for which adjustment is likely to be made include the following.

(a)   The availability of a market for the shares

By definition, all the information available about publicly-listed companies relates to shares for which a market exists, the purchaser of which is likely to be able to sell quite easily, if circumstances change and he wishes to do so. A substantial discount is normally applied in valuing a minority interest in a private company to reflect the absence of such marketability.

(b)   Premium for controlling shareholding

The values of shares listed on the Stock Exchange apply to the very small minority interests in such companies changing hands from day to day in individual transactions. Where the holding to be valued is a controlling interest, a substantial premium has to be added to recognise the advantages that a controlling shareholder enjoys when contrasted with a minority shareholder. The existence of such a premium in the market is demonstrated by the higher prices that typically have to be paid above the prevailing market level, when a public company is taken over by another.

(c)   Differences from the market generally

Differences to be taken into account between the company to be valued and the market generally or the particular companies with which comparison is being made, include: better or worse prospective earnings and dividends; higher or lower cover for dividends; greater or less exposure to business risk; possible doubts about the continuity and strength of management; and higher or lower tangible asset backing.

5.38   While it is possible to, and valuers sometimes do, attribute separate percentage adjustments to each separate factor, to do so may lend a spurious appearance of accuracy to what is ultimately a judgemental exercise, depending upon the experience of the valuer. It also has the effect of making the valuation much more readily susceptible to cross-examination. In our view, it is wiser for the valuer to say what comparisons he has made, what factors he has taken into account in the valuation of the company, and what conclusion he has reached as to the price/earnings ratio or dividend yield to be adopted, and to base his conclusion upon the application of his experience to all the relevant factors.

PARTNERSHIPS

5.39 The valuation of a partnership business may be approached on the same basis as described above, but allowance has to be made for the special characteristics of the partnership and, where someone other than the parties to the marriage is a partner in the business to be valued, for the terms of the partnership agreement.

5.40 Among the more important provisions of the partnership agreement will be what, if any, payment is made for goodwill by or to partners joining and leaving the firm. Where the partnership agreement is silent on this subject (or non-existent) the assumption to be made is that each partner owns a share in the goodwill proportionate to his interest in the profits of the firm. However, his ability to realise his interest in the firm is likely to depend on the willingness of other partners to buy him out or the availability of new partners acceptable to the continuing partners.

5.41 It is assumed for this purpose that the partnership business is of sufficient substance that its value does not fall into the *B v B* category, ie its value is not just the capitalised value of the partners' earnings capacity (see para **5.5** above). Many very substantial partnerships carrying on professional services businesses exclude in their partnership agreements any payment for goodwill and it is usual in such cases to treat the value of their interest in the partnership as being the amount that would be paid to them in respect of their capital or other accounts with the firm if they were to retire from it.

SOLE TRADERS

5.42 Most businesses of sole traders will fall into the *B v B* category referred to above in which the valuation of the business, separately from the earning capacity of the party who runs it, is of little or no significance. We have, however, encountered cases where a husband had a number of businesses, one or more of which was carried on as a sole trader, and, in considering what provision might be made for his wife, it was reasonable to contemplate that one or more of these businesses might be disposed of.

5.43 Where a business which is carried on as a sole trader employs a substantial number of people and could reasonably be expected to be carried on by someone else in succession to the existing owner, it can be seen that it would have a market value and that that value might be relevant to a consideration of the available resources. The usual approach in such cases would be to establish the appropriate level of profits upon which to base the valuation and then apply a multiplier to it. A multiplier would typically be somewhat lower than would apply to a limited company, reflecting the additional risks attaching to carrying on business without the protection of limited liability.

Chapter 6

THE CLIENT AS SHAREHOLDER, DIRECTOR OR EMPLOYEE

INTRODUCTION

6.1   It will often be a feature of a case involving either a family company or business, or one in which both parties have an interest, that problems will arise in relation to the continued running of the business, against the background of matrimonial discord and litigation. It is a rare couple who can resolve their personal problems, and continue to work together effectively and without friction in a business context, whilst in the process of dissolving their marriage. In some cases, of course, spouses simply cannot afford not to keep the business going, but that in turn creates immense pressures.

6.2   A wide range of problems can arise, including, for example, demands for resignations from office, for the termination of employment, for the sale back of shares, and for removal of the right of signature on the bank mandate; a predictable reluctance to continue to accept obligations under guarantees; disputes about the payment of dividends or repayment of loans; concerns about accruing overdrafts, and many others.

6.3   In the midst of this, each spouse will need a clear view of what they are trying to achieve and careful accountancy and legal advice (not necessarily from a specialist family lawyer) may be required. The following questions are among those which must be addressed.

–   Is the business capable of being salvaged, for the benefit of the entire family and, if so, how can this be achieved?
–   Should the status quo be preserved, and are the parties capable of working towards that objective?
–   If there are other directors, can they assist? If not, should others now be appointed?
–   Would it be better for one spouse to resign and cease to be involved and, if so, what terms need to be agreed to make that work?
–   Are there formal steps to be taken to record the new arrangements; board minutes; contractual revisions; resignations; announcements for customers, clients, investors etc?
–   Are all rights being reserved or are binding agreements being planned?
–   Will the interim financial arrangements work sensibly and practicably for the family?
–   Is the business capable, ultimately, of being divided and, if so, what preliminary investigations are needed?

– Is it essential to litigate, and to involve other jurisdictions, or with good
  advice could matters be resolved around the boardroom table?

RELEVANT DOCUMENTS

6.4   The first step, if there is time, is to ensure that, before advising the client
on any of these issues, copies of all the relevant documentation or as much of it
as possible are obtained. This should include the Memorandum and Articles of
Association of the company, together with any recent important resolutions;
the shareholders' agreement or partnership agreement, if one exists; service
contracts and terms and conditions of employment (with particular reference
to any restrictive covenants and termination provisions); any shareholder or
partnership loan documentation; banking details including any guarantees,
legal charges, bank mandate forms, and banking correspondence; any other
guarantees given in respect of business obligations such as a property lease; any
documentation relating to share transfers or the placing of shares in trust; and
up-to-date information concerning the finances of the business, including
outstanding liabilities, the tax position, the bank overdraft if there is one, the
value of fixed assets, details of stocks, debtors and cash, and a general prognosis
for future trading.

6.5   Obviously it is not essential to have all this background information in
order to advise the client on every issue, but the more that is obtained, the more
comprehensive the advice is likely to be, and indeed the better able the
practitioner will be to anticipate the problems the client may face in the future,
and to set those in the context of the matrimonial proceedings.

INTERFERENCE WITH THE BUSINESS: PRESERVING THE *STATUS QUO*

6.6   One of the governing principles in this field was emphasised very strongly
in the case of *Poon v Poon* [1994] 2 FLR 857, which was notable especially for the
determination of Thorpe J to ensure that the Family Division retained
jurisdiction over all disputes regarding the function or control of a family
company. He was confronted with the submission that any such dispute should
be resolved in the Companies Court, and that the Family Division had no
jurisdiction to invade that territory; he rejected it as 'unrealistic and contrived'.
He went on to say: 'This is a family business which the family chose to
incorporate. All current disputes within the family should be litigated in this
one court'. His judgment related specifically to a family business in which all
the shareholders were related by either blood or marriage. It may not be quite
so easy to exclude the involvement of other jurisdictions when that is not the
case.

6.7   The case arose from an application by the husband seeking orders restraining his wife from placing proposals or resolutions before an extraordinary general meeting of the company convened for the following day; her proposals involved the removal of the husband as company secretary and managing director, his replacement as secretary by an independent professional and as managing director by the wife, and the appointment, as directors, of the wife's current husband, an independent professional and the former general manager of the company. The judge detected what he called 'a clear thread of strategic manoeuvring in the various steps that had been taken by the wife and in their timing'. He reiterated the principle that, in the Family Division, pending the final hearing, every effort is made to preserve the status quo and discourage or prevent either spouse from a pre-emptive strike. On that basis he regarded it as 'unthinkable' that the wife should be allowed to go ahead to emasculate the husband's control of the company. Having said that, it is worth noting that the relief was granted to the husband on the basis of his undertaking to comply with the wife's request for the appointment of an independent director to join the board, for a professional company secretary to take over his functions, and accepting in principle the appointment as director of the new husband. One can see that, on that basis, the wife's attack was not, as strategic manoeuvres go, without success.

6.8   In contrast to the broad issues raised in this case, there are several quite specific situations which arise, and which can each be identified and dealt with separately.

EMPLOYMENT AND DIRECTORSHIP

6.9   It is necessary to distinguish between the client's position as employee and director. Employment is obviously the relationship under which full-time or part-time service is provided in return for remuneration, and the termination of any employment must be effected in accordance with the contract of employment and the relevant employment legislation (see below).

6.10   Directors have the ultimate responsibility for managing the business of a company, but their main obligation is to attend board meetings and it is not by itself a full-time position or one for which any payment will automatically be received. A client may be an executive director, which means he is both a director and employee, or non-executive, where he has no employment position. A director may resign but can only be removed by the company if the correct procedures are followed under its Articles of Association and the Companies Acts, and this usually requires a shareholders' meeting of the company. Being secretary of a company is also a separate office under the Companies Acts, but a secretary has few obligations and can resign or be removed by the directors at any time.

Resignations

6.11 Resignations of officers (as director and secretary) can be signed and become effective immediately upon delivery. However, if the client's resignation is a matter of personal choice, because for particular reasons he wishes to leave the company immediately, then it is preferable to establish that notice of the resignation has been properly filed at Companies House.

6.12 If possible, a resignation letter from an officer or employee should be given in return for a waiver by the company of any claims it might have against the officer or employee. (This would be subject to s 310 of the Companies Act 1985.) Conversely, the company may ask for a waiver of claims from the officer or employee. Care should be taken to consider such matters as outstanding bank guarantees or other guarantees or indemnities given by the officer or employee, any statutory or contractual employment entitlement and any outstanding remuneration, dividends or expenses that may be payable. No blanket waiver of rights should be given while any such matters remain outstanding.

Removal of a director

6.13 When contemplating the removal of a director, it must be ascertained from the Articles of Association whether this is a matter for the shareholders or whether the board can force a director to be removed, for example by a unanimous resolution of the other directors. If, as is usual, it is a matter for the shareholders, bear in mind the provisions of ss 303 and 304 of the Companies Act 1985 which will apply in addition to any specific provisions in the Articles, permitting the shareholders to remove a director. In summary, a company may remove a director under s 304 by ordinary resolution, notwithstanding anything in the Articles, or any agreement between the company and the director. However, special notice is required of a resolution to remove a director under s 304, and on receipt of the notice of an intended resolution the director may make representations to the company and the company will generally be required to circulate those to its members. It is a messy business and best avoided if possible. The timescale dictated by these requirements also obviously means that these steps cannot be taken instantly; in the absence of other provisions in the Articles permitting speedy removal, or an agreement to resign, a negotiated departure is much to be preferred.

TERMINATION OF EMPLOYMENT: POINTS FOR CONSIDERATION

Statutory rights

6.14 It is important to bear in mind in this context when dealing with a termination of employment (or directorship), that a spouse's employment rights whether under statute or contract (or rights to compensation for loss of office as director) are quite separate from any matrimonial claim. They will exist as between the business and the employee and it is important for both parties to ensure that those claims are resolved if possible at the time of the departure, or that everyone is aware that these issues remain outstanding. Running an industrial tribunal claim alongside an ancillary relief application will only add to the costs, but it can and does happen. The recent increase in the compensation level to £50,000 and the continuing extensions of the levels and scope of employee protection will only encourage the use of this option. If in doubt, take specialist advice.

Contractual rights

6.15 Clearly, if it is intended to dismiss an executive spouse as an employee (which may be perfectly proper), or where acting for a dismissed spouse, it is necessary to consider the possible heads of claim under the terms of any employment or service contract, and to seek full professional advice on those issues. Bear in mind, also, the opportunities for a tax-free ex gratia payment, in the correct circumstances, although the Inland Revenue are looking closely at this. Again, be sure to take specialist advice in what is an increasingly complex area.

Other benefits

6.16 Such matters as salary, bonuses, company car, pension rights, medical insurance, subsidised loans, profit-sharing schemes, share option schemes, and other perks such as subsidised accommodation or meals, all need to be considered and evaluated in any comprehensive compensation package. Many of these will, by nature, overlap into the matrimonial arena, and consideration of all relevant points may prove to be extremely complicated.

Pension rights

6.17 Very careful consideration has to be given to pension rights; some schemes may include enhanced rights where there is a dismissal or a redundancy. Bear in mind that if the parties are intending to reach agreement or litigate in the matrimonial context, in relation to the nomination of pension scheme benefits, then it may well be to their mutual advantage to ensure that they both continue to be employees until that nomination is made.

Share options

6.18 The practitioner may also have to deal with share option schemes. In some cases, these contain provisions whereby any employment termination will cause the option to lapse and will prevent the employee from including the loss of a right to benefit under the option as a head of claim for wrongful dismissal; it may not always help to trigger that. Some schemes provide that the employee will retain the right to exercise the share options already granted until the normal expiry date or for a short period after their departure, subject to the rules of the scheme and the performance criteria for exercise. Always ensure that the tax implications of exercising options are fully understood and included in any computation.

Authority to dismiss

6.19   Careful consideration should be given to the issue of who has the authority to dismiss the employee spouse and make the other decisions referred to above. Will it always be the other spouse, and is that the wisest choice? Ensure that if this step is taken, it is done properly on the basis of professional employment law advice, which may not be available from the family law specialist advising in other fields.

Compromise agreements

6.20   Finally, on the issue of termination and dismissal generally, bear in mind in particular the growth of European law in this field and the provisions under the Trade Union Reform and Employment Rights Act 1993 for compromise agreements, which must be entered into in writing and on the advice of an independent legal adviser.

SHAREHOLDERS AND TRANSFERS OF SHARES

6.21   If the departing spouse holds shares in the company, consideration will have to be given to the question of their long-term ownership. The provisions of the Articles of Association should be ascertained. It is not usual for a company to be able to require a spouse to transfer shares, but the spouse may wish to do so, or it may be in the interests of the company or the other shareholders to offer to buy those shares. Occasionally, the Articles will have been specifically drafted to provide that a shareholder who ceases to be a director or employee must offer his shares to the other members. There might also be a share-holders' agreement requiring such an offer. Remember that any compulsory transfer of shares will be subject to the court's jurisdiction to deal with matrimonial property.

6.22   If the departing spouse is a shareholder, and his or her shares cannot be bought in, then subject to any pre-emption rights which may apply and in order to protect the position, an interim shareholders' agreement may be required providing that the departing party will not sell or otherwise dispose of any beneficial interest in his or her shares for a certain period of time, and will only deal in those shares with the agreement of the board or under such constraints as may reasonably be required. Shareholdings will be matrimonial property, and unless there is good reason otherwise, they should be preserved in place until the hearing, when a property adjustment order can be made in respect of them. Again, tax implications and any reliefs which may be available should always be considered.

CONTINUING OBLIGATIONS

6.23 There is a serious risk that a departing director, partner, shareholder or owner of a business, ceasing to have further involvement in it, will be obliged to bear continuing personal liabilities, possibly in relation to company debts, unfulfilled contracts with third parties, outstanding litigation, or other liabilities from which no release can be obtained. Having departed, they will have no control over the manner in which the business is conducted and may lose touch with its affairs. Inevitably, that can be a considerable disadvantage; care needs to be taken in the decision-making process. Whilst the client remains a director, then he or she will always have the right to see the accounts, to attend board meetings, see the minutes and board papers and inspect the other books and records of the company, and thus to be kept reasonably informed. He or she may possibly have the right to sign, or refuse to sign, the accounts.

6.24 Equally, however, it must be remembered that the liabilities and obligations of company directors under present legislation are heavy. A director owes fiduciary duties and duties of skill and care to the company. There are an increasing number of statutory obligations on directors (eg accounts, taxation, health and safety). A director may be personally liable to creditors for wrongful or fraudulent trading where the company becomes insolvent. The responsibilities of being a director should not be taken lightly and, for many spouses (especially those who were never heavily involved in the business), it may be a relief to relinquish them.

BOARD MEETINGS AND SHAREHOLDERS' MEETINGS

6.25 Consideration should also be given as to whether it is constructive or necessary for a departing spouse to continue to attend company meetings (board or shareholders'). Perhaps, as has been suggested above, they should be advised to remain involved in the running of the business at some level or take responsibility for its commercial and financial obligations in order to protect their own position. It may be a better idea for them to stay informed, but to do so by appointing a professional alternate or proxy to attend the meetings on their behalf.

SIGNING THE ACCOUNTS

6.26 A refusal to sign the accounts can sometimes be used as a bargaining tool, especially if the time for filing them or submitting them to the Inland Revenue is running out. If there are genuine concerns about the contents of the accounts, then they should be addressed to the auditors, if necessary through professional advisers, and resolved if possible. If the refusal to sign is likely to cause serious problems and penalties for the business, then the value of non co-operation becomes less obvious. The very strict timetables and increasing fines which the Companies Registry now imposes should also be borne in mind.

PAYMENT OF COSTS BY A DIRECTOR

6.27 A salutary tale has been noted from the journal of the Society of Trusts and Estate Practitioners, concerning a solicitor who agreed to split his bill for professional services relating to divorce work between the client, a commercial company, and the trustees of the pension scheme. He was prosecuted and convicted of false accounting and struck off despite an otherwise unblemished career and excellent character references.

This is an important point to bear in mind for any solicitor who may be acting for a client in relation to his matrimonial problems, whilst continuing to act for the client's company on other issues. Keep the bills separate and ensure that they are paid appropriately.

BANKING ARRANGEMENTS

6.28 One of the issues that may need to be resolved is the question of banking obligations. Banks are normally extremely cautious when they know they are faced with matrimonial problems between their customers. Their anxieties may be compounded if those customers also run a business to which the bank is lending significant sums of money.

6.29 It would normally be optimistic to expect the bank to release one spouse from joint guarantees or legal charges in relation to the business without very good reason or alternative security, especially at a point where the matrimonial litigation is unresolved. However, it may be that they will be prepared to consider placing constraints upon the extent of the further borrowing or the liabilities for which the departing spouse can be held responsible, and where possible, steps should be taken to explore the protection that can be negotiated for a departing client in this situation. Notice can at least often be given to prevent future liability to the bank increasing.

6.30   A refusal by a departing spouse to agree to a change of bank mandate, removing themselves as a signatory on the business cheque-book, may also offer some negotiating scope, but a sensible bank (especially where the board of the company is in proper control of affairs) is likely to take a pragmatic view, and will be relatively reluctant to allow the business to get into difficulties simply for that reason. Taking the broad view of Thorpe J in *Poon* (see para **6.6** above), it is unlikely that any family court will be sympathetic to a spouse who seeks to exert unreasonable and detrimental commercial restraints in a process of 'strategic manoeuvring' which will cause major difficulties for the running of the business, significantly alter the status quo and possibly damage its long-term value for both parties.

ENFORCEMENT AGAINST AN OVERSEAS COMPANY

6.31   In the case of *McGladdery v McGladdery* [1999] 2 FLR 1102, CA, the court acknowledged the impossibility of enforcing orders against an overseas company established by a wife who was already bankrupt and who was determined to place whatever remaining assets there were outside the husband's reach.

The parties each owned 35 per cent of the family company, and the remaining 30 per cent was owned by a merchant bank. The wife petitioned for divorce, removed the husband as a director and dismissed him, but the financial order was made explicitly on the wife's obligation to discharge debts to the husband's family, requiring him to transfer 16 per cent of the company shares to her, on the payment of a lump sum. The wife was also ordered to pay periodical payments to the husband. She paid the lump sum and the husband transferred the shares, but she failed to discharge the debts or to make any periodical payments.

She then created a company in the British Virgin Islands to which she transferred all the assets of the family company, leaving the other shareholders, the husband and the bank with nothing. Shortly afterwards the family company went into liquidation, the wife was declared bankrupt, and she went to live in Monte Carlo.

6.32   The husband sought remedies against her, but his application failed and the Court of Appeal confirmed the decision. The court accepted that the wife had flouted the order and then prevented its enforcement, but it was nonetheless a final order and on the payment of the lump sum and transfer of shares, all the other applications for financial provision were dismissed. The obligation to pay the debts to the husband's family was a recital only and the order itself could not be revisited.

The court concluded that it could not set aside the transfer of the family company's assets to a company in her sole ownership because in making the transfer she had not divested herself of any assets, but had merely enhanced her own assets at the expense of other shareholders.

In his judgment Thorpe LJ added the following passage:

> 'Ideally in cases in which the husband and wife are the sole shareholders in a private company or the majority shareholder in a private company, the court's final determination of the ancillary relief applications will leave one in absolute control and the other fully compensated. But there will, of course, be cases in which available alternative assets are not sufficient to allow the party who is to have future control to acquire all the shareholding of the other. In that instance the ordinary safeguard for the spouse with a remaining minority shareholding but no control is the reality that the party with control has even greater incentive to increase the value of the trading concern. In a case such as this, where the wife seemingly resorts to dishonourable tactics, the fact that the Family Division does not have continuing jurisdiction to intervene seems to me not to be of serious consequence since there is an obvious remedy in the Companies Court which has not seemingly been exercised in this case by either the husband or by 3i, although the husband plainly knew his way to that court since, as I have related in the history, in 1995 he did make an application complaining of his wrongful exclusion. So although there seems to be a certain impotence in the Family Division to do justice, there is at least a remedy in the Chancery Division.'

6.33   The Court of Appeal also considered the husband's application to set aside the transfer of the assets to the BVI company, but that too was rejected. The transfer was made by the family company, which could not be regarded as the *alter ego* of either spouse, and the fact that it was a transfer made to the *alter ego* of the wife was immaterial. If the husband had no claim as spouse, then his claim as a minority shareholder could only be pursued in the Chancery Division.

There was a further important point on the issue of whether or not a court could order a bankrupt former spouse to transfer property to another spouse. Thorpe LJ's conclusion was that a property adjustment order cannot be made against a bankrupt former spouse because the property of the bankrupt vests in the trustee in bankruptcy against whom any order could not be made. There is, however, power to order a bankrupt former spouse to pay a lump sum to the other spouse in very exceptional circumstances.

The background history of this case demonstrates the extent to which a spouse seeking to remove assets from the jurisdiction and working within a corporate structure may succeed in doing so. In that sense it is both worrying as well as instructive. Whilst it may be argued that the Court of Appeal was less than robust in its approach, the case clearly provides a lesson to all practitioners that care must be taken in examining the corporate structure in any case where there is a risk that steps such as those taken by this wife could be effective. The option of an application in the Chancery Division may have to be considered alongside an application for ancillary relief and thorough advice on all aspects of the issue should be obtained at the earliest possible stage.

6.34 The recent case of *Mubarak v Mubarak* [2001] 1 FLR 698, CA, highlighted the difficulties facing a court seeking to enforce a lump sum order against a husband's companies, rather than against the husband himself. Following a hearing at which the judge awarded the wife a lump sum payment of £4,875,000, the husband failed to pay the first instalment of £3,200,000, and the wife issued a judgment summons in conventional form. After some debate the judge ordered the wife to serve on the husband a document setting out the evidence on which she intended to rely, together with a concise summary of her case. In that she stated simply that the husband had not paid the lump sum he had been ordered to pay, and in a judgment at first instance which considered the court's inability to enforce the lump sum order against the husband's company, the judge nevertheless made an order on the judgment summons committing the husband to prison for six weeks, not to be enforced if the husband paid. The husband appealed the committal order, arguing that the judgment summons procedure was not Human Rights Act 1998 compliant, and the appeal was allowed in the Court of Appeal. Its conclusion was that the operation of the Human Rights Act 1998 would require the court to reconsider all the issues raised in an original relief action, because of the application of a much higher standard of proof given that the procedure subjected the respondent to the risk of the criminal sanction of imprisonment and was therefore a criminal proceeding.

Although that represents an important (and somewhat unhelpful) ruling, the issues which are more directly relevant to this text were canvassed below in the High Court before Bodey J who had to deal with the extent to which the 'corporate veil' operated by the husband could be lifted, and the court enabled to make orders directly against the company where the company or its assets had been formed or used as a device or sham.

Bodey J concluded that even where a spouse conceded that the assets of the company could be treated as his own, the court could only lift the corporate veil and make orders directly or indirectly regarding the company's assets where: (i) the spouse was the owner and controller of the company concerned; and (ii) there were no adverse third party interests. Lifting the veil was most likely to be acceptable where the asset concerned was the party's former matrimonial home, or some other asset owned for purposes other than day-to-day trading. In this case, both companies were bona fide trading companies, the husband was a director of one, but not of the other, and there were genuine third party rights and interests in the form of commercial creditors and directors with fiduciary duties, which ought to be respected. The corporate veil could not be lifted.

Bodey J, in a detailed judgment, reviews the two strands of authority carefully, those cases decided in the company/commercial sphere and those decided in the family sphere, and concludes that:

> 'Ideally the Family Division and the Chancery Division should plainly apply a common approach. However, the fact remains that different considerations do frequently pertain: the company approach on the one hand, being predominantly

concerned with the parties at arms length in a contractual or similar relationship; the family approach, on the other hand, being concerned with the distributive powers of the court as between husband and wife applying discretionary considerations to what will often be a mainly, if not entirely, family situation.'

He commented that, in practice, especially in the bigger cases, the husband would often make a concession that the company/trust assets could be treated as his and the case would proceed on that basis. Nevertheless, difficulties remained when the lifting of the veil was appropriate as a means of enforcement in ancillary relief proceedings and he therefore concluded that the Family Division could only make orders directly or indirectly regarding a company's assets in the situations defined above.

This does not give great encouragement to parties seeking a share of family assets which comprise predominantly genuine trading company shareholdings. Even where concessions may be made for the purposes of proceedings, the ability to enforce, and the need, until effective enforcement, for security to remain in place, become increasingly significant. This case, and the *McGladdery* case do not make encouraging reading for, in particular, wives of husbands whose assets are almost entirely composed of their business shareholdings, whatever concessions they may apparently be prepared to make in the course of the proceedings.

BUSINESS BORROWINGS: CHALLENGING THE BANK GUARANTEE OR MORTGAGE; *O'BRIEN* AND OTHERS

6.35   In recent years, there has been a significant increase in the number of litigated cases between banks/building societies on the one hand and home-owner customers on the other, in circumstances where the customer and/or the customer's spouse has sought to challenge the validity of the loan facility and resist enforcement by the bank. This has occurred with the greatest frequency in the context of business borrowing.

6.36   It is a common scenario for the practitioner; the client (often the wife) tells you that the matrimonial home has been charged as security for her husband's guarantee to his company's bankers for loans afforded to that company. The wife says that she did not really read the documents; that she had signed them because her husband had told her to do so (usually at the same time assuring her that it was 'just a formality'); that she did not know what she was signing and what the effect would be; and that she had not been asked to take independent legal advice.

6.37   The marriage has now broken down, and the client is horrified to learn that the equity in the matrimonial home is much less than she had thought, and feels that she surely cannot be bound, as the guarantee was in connection with her husband's business.

6.38   For many years this has been a difficult area for family law practitioners, involving as it does questions of undue influence, misrepresentation, constructive or actual notice thereof, and agency.

The issues have not been simplified by the high volume of important cases which have been reported over the last few years, beginning with *Barclays Bank plc v O'Brien & Another* [1994] 1 AC 180 and *CIBC Mortgages Plc v Pitt & Another* [1994] 1 AC 200, both House of Lords cases.

These, and the numerous subsequent cases, have been well publicised in the national press, in particular *Royal Bank of Scotland v Etridge (No 2)* [1998] 2 FLR 843, CA.

6.39   In that case, on the issue of getting independent legal advice, Stuart-Smith LJ observed:

> '[A solicitor's] duty is to satisfy himself that his client is free from improper influence, and the first step must be to ascertain whether [the transaction] is one into which she could sensibly be advised to enter if free from such influence. If he is not so satisfied it is his duty to advise her not to enter into it, and to refuse to act further for her in the implementation of the transaction if she persists.'

The judge also took the view that, in that event, whilst the content of the solicitor's advice would be confidential, he should nevertheless inform other parties including the bank that he had seen the client, given certain advice and declined to act any further.

The Court of Appeal set out a number of useful guidelines, including the observation that it was obviously unwise for the solicitor acting for the bank to advise the wife, although there might be no conflict of interest between husband and wife.

All these cases have been well publicised in the national press, and practitioners will continue to be approached by optimistic clients hoping to find a way of avoiding enforcement proceedings whether in the context of a matrimonial dispute or otherwise. The majority of those clients will be disappointed.

6.40   In order to assess the prospects of success, it will be essential to establish a number of key points and the following questions would therefore need to be asked (assuming for this purpose it is the wife who consults the practitioner, after the event).

– Who is the client? Is it the bank, the company, the husband/director or the wife? Does a conflict of interest arise?
– Has the wife been advised to seek independent advice and has it been given to her?
– What was the purpose of the loan and was it used for its stated purpose?
– Was the documentation signed in the presence of the husband? How or where was it signed?
– Has there been any undue influence on the part of the husband, the bank or the solicitor?

- Has the wife been fully advised as to the implications of securing business borrowings on a matrimonial home?
- Has she been advised as to whether the mortgage was an all monies charge or limited to a specific sum? Is there written evidence of this?
- Are there solicitor or bank attendance notes or correspondence confirming the advice given? Where are they? Will the adviser be able to see them without difficulty?
- Does the wife receive any direct financial benefit from the borrowing?
- Does the wife have any involvement in her husband's company – is she a director, secretary, shareholder etc?
- Has there been consistency in the defence taken in the ancillary relief proceedings and in any possession proceedings? In the recent case of *First National Bank plc v Walker* [2001] 1 FLR 505, CA, the court held that it was an abuse of process for a wife to seek a property adjustment order on the basis that a valid charge over the home had been executed whilst defending possession proceedings on the ground of undue influence.

6.41   These are fundamental questions which must be considered by anyone advising in this situation, and a failure to review the issues thoroughly undoubtedly renders solicitors vulnerable either to allegations of negligence, or professional misconduct in breaching the conflict rules.

This is a complex area of law, which has developed a jurisprudence of its own. It is not practical in this textbook to deal in detail with the issues which arise from a series of cases which now spread over almost 10 years, but it is important to emphasise that any solicitor advising a client in this situation, whether before any documents are signed or in retrospect, and whether in the context of an actual or potential matrimonial dispute or otherwise, must take extreme care.

In the absence of any other factors giving rise to notice, a bank is entitled to rely upon an assurance given by a solicitor whom the bank itself retains, that proper independent advice has been given to a borrower. The solicitor's professional duty will be to the signatory, irrespective of who pays his fee. It follows, therefore, that the unhappy signatory may have an action against the solicitor, subject of course to establishing that the breach of duty caused the financial loss suffered.

SHAREHOLDER PROTECTION; DISTRIBUTION OF DIVIDENDS

6.42   The distribution of dividends where both spouses are shareholders in the company may often have been relatively informal, with no obvious distinction drawn between the parties when they were together, even if they held shares in different proportions. Once a separation takes place then strictly the position should change. Each party should on a distribution be entitled to receive the dividends attributable to their own holding. However, where one party is a majority shareholder and remains in exclusive control of the company finances and decides upon the declaration (or not) of dividends, that may in practice be difficult to achieve.

6.43 The rather cumbersome, but sometimes quite effective, option for a minority shareholder who is suffering from such prejudicial behaviour is an application under s 459 of the Companies Act 1985, by petition for an order that the company's affairs are being or have been conducted in a manner which is unfairly prejudicial to the interests of some part of the members, or that any act or omission of the company is or would be so prejudicial. This remedy can be used to counter other prejudicial conduct, such as the removal of the spouse as a director of a company where he or she has a legitimate expectation of continuing to be involved in management; note the cases involving a quasi-partnership company.

6.44 This will bring issues surrounding the family business back into the Companies Court, but with justification. The court can make such orders as it thinks fit for giving relief in respect of the matters complained of, including regulating the conduct of the company's affairs in the future, imposing constraints upon the company or requiring it to take certain steps, and ultimately providing for the purchase of the company shares by other members or by the company itself.

6.45 As an alternative, an aggrieved shareholder may also apply to the court for the company to be wound up on the grounds that it is 'just and equitable' under s 122(1)(g) of the Insolvency Act 1986. A refusal to pay dividends and the exclusion of a shareholder from participation in the business of a quasi-partnership company have been held to be grounds for an application under this section, which if successful will have the drastic result of the appointment of a liquidator and the disposal and winding-up of the company.

6.46 The case of *Nurcombe v Nurcombe and Another* [1985] 1 All ER 65 should be borne in mind. A wife holding a minority share in the company proved her claim in the matrimonial proceedings, after it became clear that the husband had breached the fiduciary duty he owed as a director of the company by diverting a lucrative transaction to another company in which he had a controlling interest. Although this issue was not fully developed in the course of the matrimonial hearing, sufficient information emerged to enable the court to take it into account in awarding the wife her lump sum. Having received two instalments she then started a minority shareholders' action claiming that the husband should pay the improper profit received from the transaction to the company. Her action was dismissed at first instance and on appeal, on the basis that it would be inequitable to allow her to continue it, given that she had chosen to continue with the matrimonial proceedings and had received the benefit of the award in those proceedings, which had taken the husband's improper profit into account.

6.47   Clearly, where there is an overlap between corporate and matrimonial issues in cases such as *Nurcombe*, the client needs very careful corporate law advice, and should consider first what genuine grounds he or she may have for an application; and secondly, the question of whether or not an application in the Companies Court or county court would be appropriate, cost effective, and strategically sensible in the context of the matrimonial proceedings, and if and when a transfer to the Family Division might be appropriate or achievable.

THE COMPANY PENSION SCHEME

6.48   The previous edition of this book included a chapter dealing at some length with the Company Pension Scheme, much of which was dedicated to an analysis of the case of *Brooks v Brooks* [1995] Fam 70 and an explanation of the then new Pensions Act 1995. All of that has now been overtaken by the changes to the legislation introduced by the Welfare Reform and Pensions Act 1999 which will be applicable to divorces filed on or after 1 December 2000.

In proceedings commenced before that date, the earmarking orders introduced by the Pensions Act 1995 will be available, but the new legislation removes the *Brooks* option and concentrates on the sharing or splitting of a pension, giving the court an increased scope to resolve those cases where the pension may represent a substantial proportion of the family's assets which has hitherto been illiquid. The issues and the procedures are complex, and in the early stages all the participants, clients, lawyers, independent financial advisers and scheme trustees will take time to find their feet.

6.49   The costs of resolving issues in the context of ancillary relief proceedings will increase; there will be more information to seek out, there will be valuations and projections to obtain, more work for the lawyers in instructing the experts and analysing their responses, another issue to negotiate or litigate, and then to implement, and in the early stages there will be little previous experience to guide practitioners as to the approach to adopt. Add to this the fact that independent financial advisers and, in the more complex cases, actuaries will need to be involved and will in all probability be charging on a fee basis (albeit that this may be set against commission obtained on arranging an external transfer), and that, in addition, pension scheme trustees will be charging fees which could be in the region of £500–£2,000.

6.50   While this legislation may sound predominantly like good news for the traditional non-working wife who may make a claim against her husband's pension fund, it will also offer an opportunity for some husbands to create clean-break settlements and perhaps to claim a share in the matrimonial home, in a case where otherwise they might have been inclined (or obliged) to relinquish that and simply retain their pension fund. In some situations, the property will represent the only (relatively) liquid capital, whereas the pension will not be available for years to come. Wives in that situation could face a backlash.

6.51 It is possible that there may be some difficulties in small company pension schemes where the assets are not invested in a conventional way, but are represented perhaps by factory premises, an office block, or a portfolio of intellectual property rights. In those cases, an immediate pension split will not be an option or, at least, not apparently so, unless and until a sale of the asset is implemented and a notional sharing secured by an appropriate charge may be the only practical option. Those cases may cause rather more difficulty.

This is not the place to enter into a detailed analysis of the new legislation; it is complex and in its very earliest stages. There have already been a number of textbooks written about it and practitioners faced with the need to advise in this field (and most will be in due course) need to ensure that they fully understand all the issues, and that they are able to turn to experienced financial advisers and actuaries where appropriate.

GATHERING PENSION INFORMATION

6.52 It will be readily apparent that, in the context of considering the business circumstances of any spouse, the nature of the available company or other pension rights will always be a vital part of the equation. Whether the scheme is a small self-administered fund, or an occupational pension fund, the salient elements of it will need to be identified, questions will have to be asked of the trustees, documentation obtained and an accurate and comprehensive valuation prepared. The bulk of this information is in any event required for the Form E. Following this, an analysis can be carried out as to the applicability and relevance of the options now available. Where appropriate, applications for further information and directions can be made. Be sure to understand the rules in relation to service of proceedings on pension providers; this becomes increasingly important.

6.53 If the client does not have all the information which is required in order to assess accurately the nature of the scheme and its value, then it should be sought; if the position is complex and the sums involved are significant, obtain specialist advice; and if an acceptable solution is not immediately apparent, ensure that the specialist is given an opportunity to formulate one and to present the proposals to the court.

6.54 Be aware also that if a spouse has transferred from an occupational scheme to a personal pension scheme, there could be an unexpected asset in the form of a potential compensation claim where the decision to transfer was taken on bad advice. Some two million pension holders are believed to be affected by this problem.

6.55 Some commentators are questioning whether the proposed modified form of valuation – the cash equivalent transfer value – is appropriate for longer marriages or where the benefits are substantial, and have expressed concern that it may not genuinely reflect the value of the spouses' interests. These questions should be borne in mind, and there are experienced specialist advisers able to assist if need be. There are, in any event, different approaches to the calculation of the cash equivalent transfer value.

6.56 It is also essential to note that the present cash value may be rather less valuable than the amount which will be payable at or after retirement; that the transfer value will take no account of tax, and that rates may of course change before the pension falls into payment. There is also the general issue of uncertainty to be taken into account in negotiation; if, for example, the member spouse dies before reaching retirement age, or the fund diminishes, or the scheme fails. The problems associated with Robert Maxwell remain a matter of concern for many people.

6.57 Practitioners will now have a wider range of options for their clients including pension sharing, although they may still be inclined to arrange a set-off of pension values against the rest of the matrimonial property (if only for the sake of simplicity). The practitioner will have to consider whether it is better to seek an attachment order, a pension sharing order, or a cash settlement in lieu by way of a set-off, a deferred lump sum or some form of agreed nomination, a form of periodical payments provision or a pension split. The problem remains that the earmarked periodical payments will fail on the death of either party and cannot be continued as a widow's pension. That, of course, is the great attraction of the pension sharing order, which will greatly assist in achieving, in many cases, a clean break, which was not previously possible.

6.58 If in doubt about the best way forward, actuarial or other specialist consultancy advice should be sought, although again care is needed in balancing the costs against the overall situation. In the context of pension sharing more detailed information, and a range of projections, is likely to be required. It may be essential to liaise with the financial adviser or pensions specialist to establish precisely what information they will need to advise properly.

6.59 Bear in mind, finally, that a failure properly to assess the pension position renders the practitioner liable to the allegation of negligence (see *Griffiths v Dawson & Co* [1993] 2 FLR 315). The risk of this is significantly increased as a result of all the new legislation, which indicates the importance of the issue even more clearly. It will now be vital to establish the overall significance of each party's pension scheme, otherwise the loss of benefits suffered as a result of the dissolution of the marriage cannot possibly be assessed. The loss will not be just the widow's benefit, but the loss of participation in the other benefits of the scheme, the commuted lump sum and the enjoyment of the pension itself.

PARTNERSHIPS

6.60 Most of this chapter has dealt with the client as shareholder, director or employee of a business operated through a limited company. There are a number of separate issues worth noting, where the client is a partner in a business run as a partnership. In the first instance, obtain copies of relevant documents, and in particular any partnership contract or deed. It may be that there is no written agreement and that the Partnership Act 1890 will imply this to be a partnership at will.

6.61 Consideration must be given as to whether it is in the interests of the client to remain as a partner. The client may prefer to do so in order to continue to receive an income, to be entitled to share in the capital of the business, and to have access to all books and papers. Alternatively, the client may wish to retire. This may not technically be possible if there are only two partners. If there are more than two, the terms for retirement should be set out in the partnership contract. If there is no right to retire, then the client will have to consider dissolving the partnership, by using the procedure in the partnership contract or giving notice under the Partnership Act 1890 if it is a partnership at will. Dissolution is clearly a drastic step involving the winding-up of the business and the consequences (not least in relation to taxation) need to be carefully considered.

6.62 A partnership contract may entitle one partner to be expelled by the others in specified circumstances, such as serious breach of duty. This would apply only in the case of a partnership of several persons.

6.63 An outgoing partner will clearly be interested in securing appropriate financial arrangements for the payment of any outstanding share of income and for the repayment of his or her capital account. These matters may be dealt with in the partnership contract. An outgoing partner will also be concerned to minimise any exposure for pre-retirement debts and should endeavour to seek an indemnity from the continuing partner(s). This may be a reasonable and achievable request if such debts have been taken into account in computing his or her share of profits. The partnership contract may already provide an indemnity.

6.64 Finally, a departing partner should not be liable for the post-retirement debts of the partnership, provided he or she does not allow himself or herself to be still held out as a partner. Thus consideration should be given urgently to serving notice of the retirement to all clients and suppliers and possibly to the *London Gazette*, and to ensuring that the name is removed from the partnership notepaper.

WHITE: THE RELEVANCE OF PARTNERSHIP LAW?

6.65 In *White v White* (already mentioned at some length above), in the Court of Appeal, Thorpe LJ raised the issue of partnership, not previously canvassed to any significant degree in the court below. He said:

> 'The dominant feature of this case is that from first to last the parties traded as equal partners. Had the partnership dissolved by the death of either, the extent of the estate of the deceased partner would have been established according to the law of partnership. Equally, the wife was in law entitled to her share on dissolution by mutual agreement. Even after the separation the wife continued in partnership and the partnership was only dissolved as part of the process of judgment. I find it difficult to understand why in the court below the wife's advisers presented her proprietary entitlement in the way that they did.'

He went on to speculate about the way in which the wife's claim could have been put forward and there is some debate about whether this was a rigorous application of partnership law, which should have been taken into consideration by those advising the parties, or whether in fact it was with hindsight something of a red herring. Lord Nicholls in the House of Lords was not uncritical of the approach. He also pointed out that the substantial additional evidence produced in relation to the partnership agreement in the Lords' hearing, demonstrated that if a strict valuation of their shares on the dissolution of the partnership were needed, then a whole range of disputes about related issues would have to be resolved. He clearly thought that was both unnecessary and inappropriate.

6.66 In all the circumstances, although it was undoubtedly significant background that Mr and Mrs White traded formerly under a partnership agreement, as Butler-Sloss LJ said in the Court of Appeal (perhaps subtly differing from Thorpe LJ):

> 'In a case where the spouses were in business together the starting point has to be their respective financial positions at the end of their business relationship. This may in many cases be achieved by a broad assessment of the financial position and I am not advocating a detailed partnership account.'

She went on to distinguish the partnership case where the wife was an equal partner, even if the assets were large, to those big money cases where the origin of the wealth was on one side and the emphasis was rightly on contribution and not entitlement. She pointed out that there would be partnership cases where the starting point would have to be adjusted upwards or downwards according to the circumstances of the case and whether or not there were children, and that partnership may not necessarily require equal division; any imbalance from the greater injection of capital by one party could be reflected in the proportions allocated to each party. She cautioned:

> 'Divorcing parties and their legal advisers ought to reflect upon the need to rethink the correct approach to the wife who is also in every sense the business partner of the husband.'

It is far from clear precisely where this leaves the practitioner advising the client who is in partnership, but broadly, the House of Lords appear to reject the concept that a detailed partnership account should be taken and that such an exercise would have an overriding influence against the background of the other s 25 factors. Practitioners should therefore be cautious in preparing evidence on the partnership issue and in contending that it should outweigh the 'broad assessment' of the parties' entitlement, especially if the cost of doing so would arguably offend against the principle of proportionality.

Chapter 7

RAISING FUNDS FOR THE SETTLEMENT

GENERAL CONSIDERATIONS

7.1   In the great majority of cases, there is no significant capital available after the separate housing needs of husband and wife have been taken care of. For the purposes of this chapter, however, it is assumed that a spouse (here the wife) is seeking a substantial capital sum, either by way of lump sum settlement of her entitlement to be maintained, or as a separate entitlement in addition to maintenance. Many of the considerations raised will also be relevant where the need is limited to the raising of capital to finance a home for the party who will not be occupying the former matrimonial home, or whose housing needs cannot be fully met by any reasonable basis for sharing the proceeds of sale of the former matrimonial home.

7.2   Where the wife is seeking a substantial capital sum from her husband, it may be important for her to be able to demonstrate how her claims can be met without unacceptably damaging her husband's business. The concern about avoiding, or at least minimising, damage may now be tempered by the approach in *White*, as discussed above. That is not to suggest that the court is likely to tell the husband how he is to meet a capital payment that he is ordered to make to his wife. The court will almost invariably leave that to the husband to decide. Nevertheless, it may be very important to demonstrate to the court that what the wife is seeking is achievable. In formulating proposals, it will also be important to demonstrate the tax consequence of what is being suggested. A proposal that has due regard for tax efficiency will be more attractive to the husband and his advisers as well as to the court, in the event that the matter goes to trial.

7.3   In the past the court has generally been disinclined to make an order that the husband cannot fulfil without serious disruption to his business. It remains to be seen whether, following the decision in *White*, this may change and the court will become more willing to contemplate a disposal of the business in order to enable the wife's claims to be met. The remainder of this chapter reflects the normal approach adopted by the court before *White*.

EXISTING LIQUIDITY

7.4   Clearly, the simplest situation will be where there are substantial liquid assets, in the form of bank balances and marketable securities, that can be readily made available without damaging the husband's ability to continue to run his business successfully. The tax consequences of realising investments should be capable of easy calculation and should normally be taken into account. Where the possibility exists of transferring assets into the wife's name without crystallising the unrealised capital gain (see Chapter 9, para **9.13**), it still needs to be taken into account because the capital gains tax can be expected to become payable as the investments are sold. It would be exceptional for management of the portfolio to be capable of being carried out in a manner that limited the realisation of capital gains to the amount of the annual exemption.

The effect of outside liquidity on the business assets

7.5   Cases of high liquidity are rare and when they do occur are often capable of resolution without undue difficulty once agreement has been reached on the level of the wife's entitlement. In these cases the dispute often focuses on the value of the husband's business, on the grounds that, the greater the value of the business that he is to retain, the larger the share of the liquid assets the wife may reasonably be entitled to.

7.6   Where the husband's business is a high risk one, it may be argued on his behalf that he should not be deprived of all his assets outside the business, since to do so would expose him too much to the hazards of failure. The husband's ability to run his business successfully may be seriously affected by whether he can afford to take business risks because he knows that he personally has some reserves, or whether he must change his way of conducting the business to 'play safe' because he knows that a wrong business judgement could leave him destitute.

ACCESSING THE LIQUIDITY OF THE BUSINESS

7.7   Where the husband's business has substantial liquidity and the liquid assets outside the business are insufficient to enable the wife's claims to be met, it becomes necessary to consider:

– whether the liquid assets of the business can reasonably be made available;
– if so, to what extent; and
– how the required sum can be extracted, preferably in a tax-efficient manner.

CAN BUSINESS LIQUIDITY REASONABLY BE MADE AVAILABLE?

7.8   Whether liquid assets held by the business can reasonably be made available depends, first, on the requirements of the business. The court will generally not make an order that the husband cannot fulfil without serious damage to his business. Furthermore, if the business depends on money borrowed from the bank or some other lender, the lender will often be unwilling to allow the husband to withdraw funds from the business. Since the order is made against the husband and is unlikely to specify how it is to be met, it does not have the effect of requiring a lender to permit the withdrawal of funds against its own interest.

7.9 Even if the company is not dependent on borrowed funds, it may have insufficient liquidity to enable a significant sum to be withdrawn. In marginal cases, it will be appropriate to consider the cash position of the business at various points during the year. If the balance sheet date falls at a time of above average liquidity, the funds existing in cash form at that date may be needed to finance stock and debtors at other times during the year. For example, a company with a trade that is seasonally biased with high levels of sales in the period up to Christmas may appear very liquid at 31 March if its balance sheet is drawn up at that date. But the same company might be heavily overdrawn at the end of October or November, when it had acquired the stock to meet Christmas orders but had either not yet made the sales or had not collected the resulting debts.

7.10 Conversely, a company may have selected a balance sheet date when its liquid position is at its worst (perhaps influenced by former tax consider-ations). It is therefore possible that the company has substantial liquidity at most times of the year. If that is so, it might be reasonable to suggest that its year-end peak requirement could be met by short-term borrowing. Where there is substantial liquidity in the company, the husband may contend that it is required to meet the plans of the company for future expansion. If the company is wholly owned by the husband and the immediate family (eg by the husband, the wife and trusts for their children), it might be considered reasonable that the rate of future expansion should be reduced to allow for the wife's needs to be met.

7.11 Different considerations arise when the business is not wholly owned by the immediate family. The withdrawal of funds from the business can only then be contemplated if a means can be found of doing so without harming the interests of the other shareholders or proprietors. Where such outside interests exist the effect on them will need to be specifically considered in relation to each of the means of extracting funds discussed above.

SEPARABLE ASSETS

7.12 In general, trading and manufacturing companies employ their assets in the generation of profits and the court will be reluctant to make an order that could be met only by the sale of business assets, if the business would thereby be damaged. There are, however, some circumstances in which this does not apply. Property companies are a good example. If the husband's company is a property company owning a number of separate properties, no structural damage will be caused by the sale of one property as a means of generating funds. Similarly, investment holding companies, particularly those with a portfolio of listed investments, can sell one or more investments without any adverse effects other than the reduction in the size of the remaining portfolio.

7.13   It is possible that other companies may have separable assets that can be similarly realised without damaging the remainder. A farming business may have land that is marginal to the main property and could be sold to a neighbouring farmer. A trading company may have property that is surplus to the needs of the main business. If such assets can be identified, the task of finding resources from which the wife's claims can be met will be made easier.

EXTRACTING AVAILABLE LIQUIDITY

7.14   If it can be established that money is available in the business that can be extracted without damage to it, the main consideration then will be to achieve the desired result in a tax-efficient way.

Loans from the husband

7.15   If the husband has lent money to the business, there should be no adverse tax consequences of repaying the loan and this will usually be the most fiscally effective means of withdrawing money up to the limits of the balance on the loan account. Even where the liquid position of the business makes repayment of such a loan difficult, it may be more tax efficient for the husband to withdraw the loan and to take out a new personal loan which he then injects into the business (see Chapter 9, paras **9.20** *et seq*).

7.16   Alternatively, the company may be able to borrow the money required to repay the husband's loan. Either of these methods enables the interest on the borrowing to be allowed as a deduction for tax. Interest on money borrowed simply to pay to the wife is not deductible for tax. Similarly, if partnership capital or the capital of a business carried on as a sole trader has been provided, otherwise than from a qualifying loan, it would be more tax efficient to withdraw capital from the business and refinance it by taking out a qualifying loan than it would be simply to borrow money to meet the wife's claims.

Loans to the husband

7.17   There are restrictions on the ability of a company to lend money to a shareholder, as well as adverse tax consequences. These are discussed in Chapter 9. In general terms, it is unlikely that a substantial capital sum can be raised, either tax efficiently or at all, by borrowing money from the company.

These restrictions do not apply to unincorporated businesses carried on by a sole trader or in partnership. Money may be withdrawn from or lent back to the proprietor or partner. However, there may be tax consequences if the effect will be to reduce the amount of a qualifying loan for tax purposes (see Chapter 9, paras **9.25** *et seq*). So far as a partnership is concerned, it will also be necessary to consider the interests of the other partners and the requirements of the partnership agreement, if any.

Increasing the husband's income to enable outside borrowings to be serviced

7.18   If substantial capital is not proposed to be withdrawn from the business, it may be suggested that the husband should borrow from outside the business to meet the wife's claims and that his income from the business should be increased to enable the loan to be serviced. This might be done either by increasing the husband's remuneration from the business or by the payment of an increased dividend by a company carrying on the business.

Directors' remuneration
7.19   An increase in directors' remuneration will carry with it not only an increased tax liability but also an increase in National Insurance. Consideration will also need to be given to the remuneration of other directors. If it became necessary to increase all directors' remuneration *pro rata* in order to provide the husband with the additional income required, the cost might be beyond the ability of the company to pay, even though the increase in the husband's remuneration alone would have been affordable.

7.20   This problem may exist even where the company is wholly owned by the husband. In an unreported case, the business was in a situation of high risk, with a good chance of breaking through to greatly increased profitability but a financial need to conserve funds while the expected major order for the company's product was awaited. It was clear that the other working directors, even though they had no shareholding, depended for their livelihood on the prospective success of the company and would have been seriously concerned if money had been withdrawn, by whatever means, to meet the wife's claims. Eventually these were resolved in a manner that avoided any withdrawal of funds from the company.

Dividends
7.21   Similar considerations apply to an increase in dividends, save that no National Insurance is payable on dividend income. While the rates of tax are the same for both earned and unearned income, it may sometimes be more fiscally efficient to take income as dividend income than as directors' remuneration. The combined effect of income tax, corporation tax and National Insurance need to be carefully considered in each case. In the days of investment income surcharge, the dividend route was fiscally inefficient and may again become so under a future fiscal regime.

7.22 In principle, an increase in the dividend income of one shareholder cannot usually be achieved without increasing the dividend payable to all shareholders of the same class (and possibly also to holders of other classes of shares ranking ahead of them). It is theoretically possible for the other holders to waive their entitlement to the increased dividend, but this would be unlikely in practice except possibly for close members of the husband's family. Even then, they are unlikely to agree to such action prospectively and could be expected to resist any such suggestion from the wife's advisers. In the event that any shareholders do agree to waive their entitlement to all or part of a dividend, it should be borne in mind that the waiver should be executed before the dividend is declared or the shareholders may be left in the worst possible position by having to pay tax on the dividend that they have waived.

Partnership drawings
7.23 Whether partnership drawings can be increased will depend on the terms of the partnership agreement. No increase in National Insurance would result but the interests of other partners may conflict with the wish of the husband (or of his wife) that his drawings should be increased beyond any level that may have been agreed.

Purchase by a company of its own shares

7.24 In some circumstances, the possibility may exist that the company could buy back its own shares from one or more shareholders. This has the attraction that money flows only to the shareholder or shareholders whose shares are being acquired. The other shareholders are not usually adversely affected since the proportions of the capital of the company represented by their shareholdings are all increased. This route may be particularly attractive where the wife holds shares in the company and it is desired that she should give up her holding as part of the capital settlement. It is also a possibility where the husband has a majority shareholding which would be diluted by selling some of his shares back to the company without depriving him of control.

7.25 The tax consequences of a purchase by a company of its own shares are referred to in Chapter 9, paras **9.33** *et seq.* The company law requirements are set out in full in ss 162 *et seq* of the Companies Act 1985. The main requirements are:

(a) the company's Articles of Association must permit it;
(b) the purchase must be made out of distributable profits;
(c) assuming that the company's shares are not listed or dealt in on a recognised stock exchange, the purchase must be authorised by a special resolution of the company.

Purchase by pension fund of shares in the company

7.26 It may be suggested that liquidity could be made available by the purchase of shares in the family company, held by either the husband or the wife, by the company's pension fund. However, it has long been regarded as bad practice for pension funds to invest in the employer company, because of the risk that, if the company founders, its employees will be left without employment and with reduced pensions. The court is unlikely to look favourably on the suggestion that the risk to employees of the company should be increased as a means of facilitating the financial settlement of a divorce. Under the Pensions Act 1995, there are restrictions on the ability of a pension fund to invest more than 5 per cent of their assets in the employer. This method is therefore unlikely to make any significant contribution to the solution.

Sale of shares to a third party

7.27   The least probable way of raising money to meet the wife's claims is by the sale of all or part of the husband's or wife's shareholding to a third party. It is usually difficult to find outsiders who wish to invest substantial funds in a holding in an unlisted company. Even if such a purchaser can be found, it is usually unattractive to bring in to the company someone who may find himself in the position once described by a judge in another division as 'the detested intruder'.

7.28   Exceptionally, there may be a real prospect of the company's shares being listed on the Stock Exchange in the not too distant future, in which case the disposal of a minority interest to a venture capital fund or to a financial institution, such as Investors in Industry plc (3i), may be possible. In general, institutions are unwilling to invest in private companies unless they can see a real probability that they will be able to exit with a profit within a period of, at most, five years.

7.29   Even where the company's shares are listed on the Stock Exchange, it cannot always be assumed that they should be regarded as available liquid assets. In one unreported case in the High Court, the husband had a minority interest in a substantial listed company. Evidence was given on the wife's behalf that the reduction of his minority shareholding to a somewhat smaller minority holding by selling some shares to release capital to her, would have no real adverse effect on the husband's position. Nevertheless, the court accepted a submission on behalf of the husband that the shares were in the nature of working capital and should not be regarded as available to meet the wife's claims. It is doubtful whether this would be regarded as a general rule and each case probably has to be determined on its own particular circumstances.

EFFECT OF FORTHCOMING RETIREMENT

7.30   Where the husband is approaching retirement age, it becomes relevant to consider what will become of the business when he retires. If there are other members of the family actively engaged in the running of the business, it may be likely that the husband's retirement will not greatly affect the business and that it will carry on without him subject to any effect on its fortunes that his departure brings with it. However, if the business is heavily dependent on the husband and is unlikely to carry on without him, it is likely that he will either seek to dispose of it before he retires or that it will then be wound up.

7.31 Where it is envisaged that shares or business assets will be realised on the retirement of the husband, the availability of retirement relief in calculating the capital gains tax consequences of disposal should be taken into account (see Chapter 9, para **9.23**).

Chapter 8

THE HUSBAND'S HIDDEN WEALTH

THE NEED FOR FULL DISCLOSURE

8.1   The financial affairs of wealthy business people are often complex and it is unusual to find substantial, accessible, liquid assets available to meet any claims. More usually, the finances of (here, it is assumed) the husband and his business interests are interwoven in a way that makes it difficult to establish a reasonable estimate of the financial resources available to meet the wife's claims and to show how these claims can, in practice, be met.

8.2   The degree of difficulty in establishing the true financial resources in the face of such complexity depends greatly on the attitude of the husband in clarifying the position. Competent solicitors will invariably advise the husband that it is in his own interests to comply with his obligation to make full disclosure in a way that makes it as easy as possible for those advising the wife to understand the position. Problems sometimes arise when solicitors with less experience in this field fail to make this clear.

8.3   In rare cases, the husband may be so wealthy that he agrees that he can meet any reasonable order the court may make and may be relieved of the requirement to give detailed disclosure of his financial resources ('the millionaire's defence'); see Chapter 3, para **3.50**, although, following the *White* decision, it is doubtful whether this defence is still available. In all other cases, the wife's advisers need to be satisfied that they can see a complete and substantially accurate financial picture, before they can advise the wife on what her reasonable entitlement may be. Until that position is reached, the wife's advisers cannot enter into any meaningful discussion on settlement terms. If they do so, they may later face accusations that they were professionally negligent in advising the wife without first establishing properly what were the available financial resources of the parties.

8.4   Full and clear disclosure, therefore, not only meets the husband's legal obligations but brings with it the prospects of speedy resolution of the wife's claims, and less expense in the form of lawyers' and accountants' fees in achieving it. Experience suggests that busy and impatient business people want their advisers to finalise matters very quickly at minimum cost, but too often they fail to provide the time and effort required on their part for the production of a proper statement of their financial position, without which it is virtually impossible to achieve these objectives.

THE EFFECTS OF INCOMPLETE DISCLOSURE

8.5   It is a matter of regret that husbands do not always comply with their lawyers' advice to make full and clear disclosure. Some appear to believe that they will pay less in the end if they can preserve an element of uncertainty and confusion regarding their wealth and import the greatest possible degree of pessimism into those aspects of its assessment that require subjective appraisal. Sadly, such cases are not uncommon. In extreme cases, husbands have been known not just to confuse but deliberately to conceal their true financial position by omitting significant assets or misrepresenting their ownership or value.

8.6   In the case of *Newton v Newton* [1990] 1 FLR 33, the husband was aged 64 and the wife 56. The parties were married in 1959 and separated in 1977. The husband had built up a successful business as a property developer but the judge had found at first instance that his income capacity was almost impossible to ascertain because he had deployed most of his liquid capital as a source of further business development. The judge also found that he could not rely upon the husband's evidence as to his capital assets and was obliged to draw inferences from the conflicting evidence of professional witnesses. He made an order that the husband should pay the wife a lump sum of £750,000 together with her costs assessed at £150,000 and ordered payment to be made within 18 months so as to give the husband time to deal with his liquidity problem.

8.7   The Court of Appeal rejected the appeal on the basis that the judge had been entitled to make an assessment of the husband's assets and conclude that the proper sum to be awarded was £750,000. The Court of Appeal also held that in the absence of any evidence called by the husband as to the reaction of credit houses to a further credit advance, the judge had been justified in holding that it was reasonably practicable for him to find a way to pay that sum by obtaining further credit and without having to liquidate his business enterprise. Thus there was no reason to either reduce the lump sum order or make an order for periodical payments in its place. Cumming-Bruce LJ commented:

> 'there is abundant authority that in approaching difficult lump sum claims the court must take a course that will not kill the goose that lays the golden eggs and must not condemn the husband to abandon his business life.'

8.8   Further on he added:

> 'But faced with absence of any evidence as to the reaction of credit houses to a further credit advance, I take the view that the Judge was justified in holding that it was reasonably practicable for the husband to find a way to pay the lump sum and to discharge his current obligations by obtaining further credit. What security he would put up for that purpose would be for him to decide, wearing his personal or his company hat or – more probably – both of them. The judge gave time of 18 months because he was persuaded that the probability was that the husband would not be forced into the solution which the experts thought would be most tax effective, but as a result of his own business experience and judgment would find a

better way of doing it, and thus would not find that the consequences of a lump sum order was to drive his enterprises into liquidation.'

8.9 There can be little doubt that husbands occasionally succeed in reducing their wives' entitlements in this way. This is because of the financial risk that a wife has to face in incurring the costs of seeking to expose the deficiencies in her husband's evidence. If the investigations and challenges undertaken on her behalf prove unsuccessful, the assets available to meet her claims will have been reduced by the costs incurred. She and her advisers may even face judicial criticism for having wasted costs in the attempt and, if the husband is not required to pay those costs, the wife may later be disinclined to do so, when they turn out to have been abortive.

8.10 It follows that the wife's advisers must make the most careful appraisal of the prospects of success and the likely costs of achieving it before they can advise the wife that substantial costs are merited in seeking to contest the husband's statement of his financial resources. Areas of doubt can often be probed by a judiciously worded questionnaire, but a full scale accountant's investigation of the kind described later in this chapter would only rarely be justified. Where deliberate and skilful concealment of assets occurs, the costs of successfully challenging the misrepresented picture are likely to be higher and the chances of failure greater.

TYPICAL WAYS OF CONCEALING ASSETS

8.11 The vast majority of divorces concern parties whose financial affairs are very simple and are known to each other, at least in general terms. Even wealthy families are likely to have property assets the identity of which is well known, an investment portfolio and a pension fund, together accounting for the great majority of the family fortune. There may be arguments about values and how the resources should be shared, but the nature and identity of the assets is broadly known to both sides.

8.12 Cases where assets are concealed are, thankfully, rare but it is worth describing some of the means by which concealment has been attempted in cases with which we have been concerned.

– A company was omitted from the husband's assets on the ground that it did not beneficially own any assets. In fact, it owned a property which it held in trust for the husband. The husband omitted the property from his disclosure on the grounds that he was not its legal owner.
– Bank accounts overseas, particularly in tax haven jurisdictions, have been omitted from disclosure.
– A substantial sum of money was described by the husband as a pension fund. In reality, it was an entirely accessible bank account with no tax penalties on withdrawals, which the husband designated as his pension fund because he hoped that it would continue to be available to him when he retired.

– An overseas company with no Stock Market quotation was described as being of no value and on the verge of liquidation. It transpired that steps to float the company on the Stock Market were at an advanced stage.
– A property held by a manufacturing company but not used in its business was said to be of no value. In fact, it was worth over £3 million which could be realised without any effect on the company's business.
– Freehold property, paintings and various companies of which the husband was a director were owned by offshore companies in which the husband held no shares and had no legal right to acquire shares. In reality, he had the expectation of enjoying ownership rights in all these assets. The structure depended on his trust of the existing shareholders' willingness to issue shares to him whenever he requested.
– Valuable businesses were carried on by companies the shares in which were owned by Swiss discretionary trusts. The Swiss trustees asserted that the discretionary objects included people other than the parties and their children and declined to disclose the extent of the trust assets on grounds of confidentiality. Proper disclosure emerged only after the wife's accountant had estimated the extent of the expenditure being funded by the trust for the family's benefit and hypothesised about the extent of the underlying capital value if this expenditure were being borne out of income.

REASONS FOR BELIEVING WEALTH IS BEING HIDDEN

8.13 How then should the wife's advisers (for it is generally their task rather than the husband's advisers) approach the task of deciding how to advise their client, when faced with the possibility that the financial position is being understated or deliberately misrepresented? The first step must be to establish what reasons exist for believing that the financial position is being misrepresented. It is not sufficient for a wife to say, 'But I'm sure he's much richer than that'. Unless she can be more specific about the reasons for her belief, it will be hard to justify incurring the substantial costs of an investigation. The client must therefore be carefully questioned on her reasons for believing that the financial position is *substantially* different.

8.14 The greater the wife's knowledge of her husband's financial affairs, the more likely it is that she will have an accurate view of whether there has been seriously inaccurate disclosure and that she will be able to explain the grounds for this belief. Care must be taken with all such information. For example, a client may know that her husband has a Swiss bank account. It would, however, be dangerous to assume that this signifies concealed wealth. Perhaps the family take skiing holidays in Switzerland; many families have been known to maintain a modest bank account in the country where they spend their holidays.

8.15 Typical circumstances in which serious non-disclosure may reasonably be suspected are:

(a)   where the disclosed resources are inconsistent with the standard of living disclosed;

(b)   where there are known to have been substantial assets at an earlier date (eg from the sale of a business) that appear not to have been accounted for;

(c)   where the disclosure is inconsistent with documents in the wife's possession;

(d)   where, during the marriage, the husband has misrepresented his finances to the Inland Revenue and intends to maintain his misrepresentations in the matrimonial proceedings.

Inconsistency with standard of living

8.16   Where the disclosed resources are quite inconsistent with the standard of living enjoyed by the family, it must first be asked whether there are legitimate reasons why this could be so. Has there been a recent change in the circumstances of the family that would make the past an unreliable guide to the future? In 'boom' times, the family may have lived very well; in times of recession, the past standard of living may be unsustainable.

8.17   This is likely to be claimed by the husband to be the position more often than it is in reality, but consideration needs to be given to the possibility that there has in fact been a significant downturn. In the absence of such circumstances, once proceedings have been issued the first response should be to consider the Form E and prepare, before the First Appointment, a detailed questionnaire. A series of credit card statements for a period before the breakdown of the marriage is a valuable way of indicating the general standard of living.

8.18   In one case, the wife was aware that the whole family regularly ate at a good restaurant near their home and ran an account there. She recalled that the account was, from time to time, topped up from a credit card. On enquiry, it turned out that the credit card concerned was paid by an overseas subsidiary of the husband's company. A large part of the cost of maintaining the family was charged to this card and absorbed by the overseas subsidiary, but this had not been disclosed as a resource. The husband was not a director or employee of the company concerned and the expenditure appeared to have escaped the notice of the tax authorities in either country. The wife's knowledge enabled a question to be framed in such a way that the husband could not avoid disclosing the credit card statements and an increase of some 40 per cent in his effective income was able to be established.

8.19   In another case, the credit card statements of a husband pleading minimal assets and income were shown to include a payment of £780 for hand-made shoes from a famous bespoke shoe-maker. This may have helped to influence the judge to accept the wife's counsel's submissions that the husband's disclosure was not to be believed.

Inconsistency with earlier known assets

8.20   If it is known that, in the recent past, substantial assets existed, and the disclosed position appears inconsistent with the known previous position, the husband should be asked to produce a reconciliation, in approximate terms, explaining what became of the assets that are no longer disclosed. It would be reasonable to expect him to be able to do this for major assets held within the past seven years, or perhaps longer for large sums. The longer the period, the more general the reconciliation that it would be reasonable to expect the husband to be able to produce.

Inconsistency with documents in the wife's possession

8.21   It may be that the wife has obtained documents or copies of documents relating to her husband's finances. The circumstances in which such 'self-help' is permissible are discussed in Chapter 3 at paras **3.76–3.81** and in section 6 of the SFLA Guidance Note *Good Practice in Family Law on Disclosure* (see the Appendix). Where documentary evidence of this sort has been obtained, it should be carefully compared with the husband's disclosure to identify any potential areas of inconsistency. Questions asked as a result of such comparison should make clear the fact that the documents concerned are in the possession of the wife and her advisers and are available for inspection.

8.22   The possibilities of exposing concealment of assets are at their greatest where the husband works from the matrimonial home and the wife has been able to make available to her advisers extensive photocopies of documents relating to his affairs. Where the husband is aware, before swearing his affidavit of means, that the wife has such documents, the risk of his seeking to falsify the position is greatly reduced. Where, within the limits imposed by acceptable behaviour, the husband is unaware of her possession of such documents, the scope for exposing him is at its greatest. It is in these rare cases that the potential for a skilled accountant's investigation to expose the existence, and ideally the extent, of the husband's concealment of his wealth is at its greatest.

Misrepresentation to the Inland Revenue

8.23   Some husbands who have over the years consistently misrepresented their income or capital gains to the Inland Revenue, with a view to evading tax, sustain their misrepresentations when it comes to the disclosure of their financial resources in the course of their matrimonial proceedings. This may be motivated by convenience. If they have been living a financial lie for many years, it may be convenient to use the concealing structures that have been erected against the Inland Revenue to conceal the position from the divorcing wife and her advisers. Such continuing concealment is undoubtedly also motivated in some cases by fear that the Inland Revenue will become aware of the disclosures made in the course of the divorce proceedings, whether through action by the wife, or by some access on the part of the Inland Revenue to the disclosures made in the divorce proceedings.

8.24   Until recently, it has been rare for the Inland Revenue to become aware of disclosures made in divorce proceedings (notwithstanding that until the last few years both the Principal Divorce Registry and the Inland Revenue Headquarters rested within Somerset House in London!). Judges did not, it seems, regard it as necessary to expose even quite blatant tax fraud that came to their notice in the context of confidential proceedings in the Family Division. Inland Revenue personnel could obtain access to the affidavits and other documents in matrimonial proceedings only by application to the court.

8.25   In the case of *S v S (Inland Revenue: Tax Evasion)* [1997] 2 FLR 774, the Inland Revenue were sent by the brother of a divorcing wife a copy of the judgment of Wilson J in which reference was made to tax evasion. The Inland Revenue applied to the court for access to other documents in the case. Refusing this application and ordering the return of the documents wrongly supplied to the Inland Revenue by the brother, Wilson J said:

> 'It is greatly in the public interest that all tax due should be paid and that in serious cases *pour encourager les autres*, evaders of tax should be convicted and sentenced. It feels unseemly that a Judge to whose notice tax evasion is brought should turn a blind eye to it by not causing it to be reported to the Revenue. In one sense that would almost cheapen the law.
>
> On the other hand it is greatly in the public interest that in proceedings for ancillary relief the parties should make full and frank disclosure of their resources and thus often of aspects of their financial history. Were it to be understood that candour would be likely to lead – in all but the very rare case – to exposure of under-declarations to the Revenue, the pressure wrongfully to dissemble within the proceedings might be irresistible to a far bigger congregation of litigants than is typified by the husband in these proceedings, who of course resolved not to be candid in any event. False presentations by respondents in ancillary proceedings have two repercussions, both seriously contrary to the public interest: (a) either the judge remains deceived, in which case the award is likely to be inaptly low, or he perceives the deceptions, whereupon he may draw necessarily broad inferences of hidden wealth which, depending on their scale, could make the award inaptly high or indeed leave it still inaptly low; and (b) applicants are seldom minded to compromise their claims on the basis of presentations which they believe to be materially false and their stance, if justified by the court's findings, will often be upheld in relation to costs. Yet the family justice system depends upon the compromise of all but a few applications for ancillary relief.
>
> Between these two opposing public interests must the individual circumstances be weighed.'

He concluded that, because the finding of tax evasion was of the most general character based on inference rather than specific evidence of events some nine years earlier, the application should be dismissed and the Revenue should deliver up to the court all copy transcripts of the judgment in its possession.

8.26   This approach was confirmed by a subsequent decision of Wilson J in *R v R (Disclosure to Revenue)* [1998] 1 FLR 922.

Then, on 31 January 2000, Charles J gave a long and detailed judgment which
entirely changed the picture. The case was *A v A; B v B* [2000] 1 FLR 701, and
the report in Family Law Reports occupies 58 closely typed pages. The story is
an interesting one, concerning two husbands (Mr A and Mr B) and the
attempts of their respective wives over a period of seven years to obtain
disclosure and financial relief. Those attempts were blocked at every turn
despite rigorous enquiries, attempts to obtain *Anton Piller* orders in the Isle of
Man, and enquiry agents' efforts in Ireland and the Isle of Man. Eventually,
however, one link in the chain weakened, an affidavit was supplied and the
Manx Court granted *Mareva* injunctions and *Anton Piller* orders; mirror orders
were obtained in England and Jersey, and on the eve of the trial in February
1999, the husbands acknowledged the truth. The first day of trial was spent in
negotiations following which a settlement was announced to the judge as
£1 million for each wife plus indemnity costs. The order was approved.

However, thereafter came the bombshell. Charles J announced that he was
minded to report the husbands to the Inland Revenue, the DPP and the
prosecuting authorities in the Isle of Man for evasion of tax and conspiring to
pervert the course of justice. The husbands, and no doubt their advisers,
seriously shocked by this indication, requested an adjournment to brief leading
counsel and the hearing then resumed with Chancery lawyers representing
them.

In turn, the wives could see their settlement, won at great cost, disappearing
through the door in the direction of the Revenue and submitted that their
husbands should not be reported, but that the practice of the Family Division as
illustrated in the decisions of Wilson J should be maintained.

Charles J disagreed. In a nutshell, he concluded that there was strong public
interest in full and frank disclosure being made in ancillary relief proceedings,
but that this could not prevail over the stronger public interest in suppressing
tax evasion and other unlawful conduct. Thus, if evidence of tax fraud or other
illegal conduct comes to the attention of the court in such proceedings, the
court is at liberty to report the offender to the authorities, provided he has had
a proper opportunity to invoke the privilege against self-incrimination. If this
were to mean that wives would get less because tax has to be paid, then so be it; it
is in the public interest that tax is paid.

8.27 Therefore, it now seems increasingly clear that the client must be
advised that he has a duty to make full and frank disclosure; that the court may
order disclosure to public authorities in the overall public interest; and that if
the court is satisfied that there has been illegal or unlawful conduct including
evasion or non payment of tax, then the court would normally order such
disclosure.

At the present time, the wording of Form E does not inform the deponent of his
right to invoke the privilege against self-incrimination and it has been
suggested that it should indeed now do so. The implications of making a

decision to invoke privilege in the context of disclosure cannot be certain, but it seems highly likely that the court would draw the inevitable sceptical conclusion about the extent of the accuracy of the disclosure which was provided with such a caveat in place.

Charles J was incidentally assured by leading counsel, and accepted, that both husbands had made disclosure to the Revenue and, on that basis, considered it unnecessary to report them himself. He did send a draft copy of his judgment to the Manx Court, inviting its views on whether the papers should be sent to the prosecuting authorities there, but it is not known whether he received a reply.

It is understood that at least one other High Court judge has taken the step of reporting a litigant and that district judges have circulated a practice note amongst themselves echoing the effect of Charles J's judgment in this case.

8.28   This judgment raises serious and wide-ranging issues, and demands careful consideration by practitioners faced with clients for whom disclosure could create such difficulties. Invoking the right to privilege against self-incrimination is all very well, and may protect in one sense, but clearly leaves the client open to the risk of a more punitive order than might otherwise be appropriate and with no guarantee that a tax liability will not follow in due course in an event. Great care must be taken and, where appropriate, specialist advice obtained.

ACTION TO TAKE WHERE NON-DISCLOSURE IS SUSPECTED

Probing by questionnaire

8.29   Where there are good reasons to suspect that a husband's disclosure is incomplete and misleading, the first step should be to make him and his lawyers aware of that belief. This will typically be done (at the appropriate point in the procedure, or the pre-action protocol) by preparing a detailed questionnaire in which questions designed to bring out the true position have been carefully framed. If the suspicions are justified, this should lead to his lawyers' putting pressure on him to make proper disclosure. (It may be much harder to achieve this before proceedings are issued.)

8.30   In developing the questionnaire, it should be borne in mind that a husband who has embarked on a course of misleading disclosure is likely to give the minimum possible answer to each question and to treat the form of the question literally, if it is in his interest to do so. The need to overcome this reaction will make the questionnaire longer, but can be justified by the need to unearth the true position. The length and rigour of the questionnaire will be carefully reviewed at the First Appointment by the district judge, after hearing any challenges by the other side; this too needs to be borne in mind and the questions must be framed to link with the issues in the case (see para **1.47** above).

8.31 For example, the adviser may want to establish the latest financial information about the husband's company. If the questionnaire is worded 'Produce the latest audited accounts of X Limited', he is likely to respond literally and perhaps send a three-year-old set of accounts containing the minimum information (or less) permitted by the Companies Act 1985. Instead, it may be appropriate to word the question as follows:

'(a) for each of the last three accounting periods for which audited accounts are available, provide such accounts, together with the detailed trading and profit and loss account;

(b) for each accounting period since the date to which the latest audited accounts were made up, provide the most up-to-date draft accounts available, together with any other information available to the management of the company relevant to its profitability and financial position;

(c) for the period since the latest date to which draft accounts have been made up, down to the latest future date for which they are available, provide such budgets, forecasts or other estimates as are available for the information of the management regarding the estimated and prospective profitability and financial position of the company;

(d) has any information been made available to the company's bankers or other providers of finance in connection with its current and prospective profitability and net worth? If so, provide a copy of all such information made available in the past two years.'

8.32 The assistance of an accountant of suitable experience in identifying what should be asked for and in helping to frame the right questions is likely to be valuable. Particular care should be exercised in reviewing the replies to ensure that they do actually answer the question that has been asked. Prevaricating husbands are liable to provide what looks like an answer but does not actually deal with the question asked, or to answer only one part of a composite question. Identifying where this applies may provide indications of where further probing may be successful.

8.33 In cases such as these, it is often necessary to be persistent in pursuing rigorously the answers provided and asking supplementary questions where necessary. Once it can be shown that the husband's disclosure has been incomplete, the wife's advisers are likely to have the support of the court, where necessary, in requiring the questions to be properly answered, provided that they do not clearly go beyond what is reasonably necessary to 'get to the bottom' of the area of enquiry. Bear in mind, however, that the court will prefer to keep the 'supplementaries' to a reasonable level. Think hard about the first version.

Accountants' investigations

8.34 The proper use of the questionnaire procedure to elicit from the husband proper disclosure of the true position, if it can be achieved, is likely to be the most economical route to the truth. Only in very rare and exceptional cases will it be justifiable to use the additional means of an accountant's investigation. The accountant's role will usually be to review the disclosure with the other information available, such as the documents obtained by the wife, and to identify the areas where inconsistencies are apparent and then to help to draft appropriate questions.

8.35 Exceptionally, his work may extend to a review of the major movements in the husband's financial position over a period of years to see whether there are funds coming in from a source that has not been identified or money going out to an unknown destination. For this purpose the accountant will need copies of:

(a) bank statements for all bank accounts, building societies or other savings or investment institutions, annotated to show the source or destination of all receipts and payments over, say, £1,000;
(b) all accounts with stock brokers or investment managers, identifying the source and destination of all significant cash transfers;
(c) accounts with any company controlled by the husband or by which he is employed;
(d) any other account to or from which any significant cash flows have passed.

8.36 These accounts can then be reviewed to see that all significant movements of assets are accounted for and that they are consistent with the financial resources disclosed; any incomplete information can then be probed.

DEALING WITH PERSISTENT NON-DISCLOSURE

8.37 Where the husband persists in prevarication, and in providing inadequate answers to questions, so that the wife's advisers, having used the various means described in Chapter 3, are still unable to get at the true picture, it will rarely be possible to do so by direct means. The financial position of offshore companies or Liechtenstein Foundations and the existence and ownership of numbered Swiss bank accounts, for example, are usually impossible to establish and the accountant should not be expected to be able to overcome secrecy laws that have been successful in defeating fiscal authorities for very many years. Costs spent in trying to do so are likely to be wasted.

8.38 The better course is to rely on the court to use its discretion in the wife's favour, which it will do in appropriate circumstances by drawing the inference that the resources are larger than have been disclosed. The accountant should therefore be invited to prepare a report in which the husband's original disclosure is contrasted with what is now known, and in which the grounds for believing that the disclosure is incomplete are set out.

8.39 The most extreme case of this sort, with which we were concerned in the late 1980s, was one in which the husband's affidavit disclosed net assets of

£52,000, amended just before trial to net liabilities of £73,000. The husband was employed by an offshore company, and all his business interests had for many years been connected with a number of other offshore companies. He claimed to be an adviser to the company that managed these offshore companies, but no correspondence with any of them could be produced. One of the companies was known to have made a substantial profit on the takeover, some years previously, of a company of which the husband was managing director. The pictures on the wall of the matrimonial home, some of which had been chosen by the wife, were owned by an offshore company and the skiing lodge used by the family was owned by another.

8.40   Affidavits were produced and witnesses came to court in person to swear that the husband did not have and never had had any beneficial interest in the issued share capital of any of these companies nor any entitlement ever to acquire such an interest. Although the wife's advisers could prove nothing and had no way of establishing the financial position of the companies, there were some indications that there was at least £1 million in them. An accountant's report was produced, setting out the circumstantial evidence supporting the belief that the arrangements were a façade constructed to defeat the tax authorities, and explaining how the husband might be able to obtain control by a means that was not inconsistent with the evidence about the companies' ownership.

8.41   The court awarded the wife the matrimonial home and some £700,000, which the husband appeared to have no difficulty in paying. This case highlights the difficult position of the advisers in such a situation. It could be shown that almost certainly a façade had been constructed, but it could not be said with any certainty what lay behind the façade. There was a serious risk that the court might have declined to award the wife a sum that she could not demonstrate the husband possessed. In that event, the significant costs of taking the case to trial would have been unlikely to have been recoverable and the wife's limited assets would have been depleted.

8.42   In other cases of serious non-disclosure, the risk of taking the matter to trial may well be too great. Regrettably, some husbands who are clearly concealing their wealth are successful in 'bluffing it out'. If, after seeking such support as can be obtained from the court by way of orders to provide information, the wife's advisers are still unable to establish, even broadly, what the true level of the financial resources may be, it is sometimes necessary to advise the client that, although there may be substantially greater net assets than have been disclosed, the prospects of establishing the position are low in relation to the costs of trying to do so, and that it may be in her best interests to settle on the best terms available.

THE VIEW FROM THE OTHER SIDE

8.43   This chapter has dealt so far with the problem, from the viewpoint of a client and her advisers, of a spouse who fails to make full, frank and clear disclosure. What of the view from the other side? While there can be no sympathy for husbands who conceal their wealth, husbands who have told the truth but are accused of lying are entitled to full support.

8.44   Where those advising the husband are faced with non-acceptance by the wife of the fullness of disclosure which the husband claims is complete, urgent action is needed to avoid the risk that the wife's advisers will incur unjustified costs in trying to prove the existence of assets that do not exist. If this cannot be achieved, regardless of any award that the court may eventually make, the husband will not, in practice, be insulated from the resulting depletion of the parties' combined resources. The husband's advisers should point out to the wife's advisers the consequences in terms of costs, but this must be done in such a way that it does not appear to be an attempt to bully them out of legitimate lines of enquiry.

8.45   There is a serious danger that the emotions between the parties may be raised to such a level that a written 'slanging match' ensues between them and/or their advisers. It is crucial to respond calmly and rationally. In practice, advisers with the task of convincing the other side that there are no hidden assets are faced with the difficult task of proving a negative, and there are no certain, low cost, ways of doing this.

8.46   The first step should be to review carefully the husband's disclosure, to see whether there are areas that are not as clear as they should be and could be clarified; to suggest reasons why these beliefs have been formed by the other party; and to determine whether there are any other documents that could be put forward by way of corroboration. If the husband has an existing accountant who is fully aware of his financial position, every effort should be made to arrange for an early meeting between the husband's accountant and the wife's so that he may seek to persuade the latter that his approach is misguided by listening to his reasons for disbelieving and seeking to refute them with reasoned responses.

8.47   If there is no existing accountant who can do this, a specialist accountant may need to be called in to review all the sources of information available and produce a financial report. He should then seek an early meeting with his counterpart to try to allay the unjustified allegations of misrepresentation. To the extent that these meetings are open, rather than 'without prejudice', a note should be made and agreed between the accountants of what was said, so that there should later be no argument in this regard.

Chapter 9

TAXATION

INTRODUCTION

9.1   Although this book is concerned mainly with matters relating to business assets, this chapter also sets out a number of personal tax issues to be considered in the context of the settlement of the financial applications of the parties. The following sets out the basic principles of taxation relating to married couples under the current system and some of the specific areas that need to be considered when a marriage breaks down.

THE DATE OF SEPARATION OR DIVORCE

9.2   For income tax and capital gains tax purposes, it is important to establish the date on which a married couple separate. For these two taxes this is the key date rather than the date of the divorce. For inheritance tax purposes, however, the date of the decree absolute may be of significance as the inter-spouse exemption will cease to apply on that date (see below).

9.3   Although husbands and wives are generally taxed separately, whether they are separated or living together is relevant for a number of reasons, for example, whether transfers of assets can be made between spouses on a 'no gains/no loss' basis or, if one of the parties was over 65 on 5 April 2000, whether the married couple's allowance is due.

9.4   A couple are treated as living together unless they are:

(a)   separated under an order of the court;
(b)   separated under a deed of separation; or
(c)   in fact separated in circumstances such that the separation is likely to be permanent.

INCOME TAX: ALLOWANCES

Personal allowances

9.5   Under current legislation, every individual is entitled to a personal allowance which, for the year 2001/2002, amounts to £4,535. This allowance is not affected by the marital status of the claimant and continues to be due to each party to the marriage following separation and divorce. Relief is available at the individual's highest rate of tax. The married couple's allowance was abolished with effect from 2000/2001 for those individuals who were under 65 on 5 April 2000.

9.6 A higher personal allowance and married couple's allowance may be available to individuals who are over 65 at some point during the tax year. The level of the allowance depends on whether the claimant's total income exceeds specified limits. Since 1993/94, a wife has been able to elect to claim one half of the married couple's allowance (in those cases where it is still available) for any year of assessment, the husband's entitlement being reduced accordingly. Alternatively, they may jointly elect for the wife to be able to claim the full amount of the allowance. In the year in which the couple separate, the allowance can continue to be claimed in full and can reduce the claimant's income tax liability regardless of whether the income arose before or after separation.

Additional personal allowance

9.7 The additional personal allowance, formerly available to single parent families, has been abolished with effect from 6 April 2000.

Children's tax credit

9.8 With effect from 6 April 2001, the children's tax credit has been introduced. This is given to families (including single parent families) with one or more children and will be an allowance of £5,200, with relief normally given to the higher earner in the family unit. The credit is tapered so that £2 of tax relief will be lost for every £3 of income above £29,400 until the credit is exhausted.

TAXATION OF MAINTENANCE PAYMENTS

9.9 Until 5 April 2000, tax relief continued to be available for most maintenance payments arising from orders or agreements made before 15 March 1988. From 6 April 2000 this relief has been abolished.

Maintenance payments have been removed from the taxation system. Tax is not deducted at source and the payments do not form part of the taxable income of the recipient.

SECURED MAINTENANCE

9.10 In some cases the payer of maintenance cannot be relied upon to meet his obligations and, in order to ensure the payee receives what is due to her, secured maintenance payments may have to be put into place. A common way of dealing with this is for the payer to transfer income-producing assets to a trust from which the payee will receive the maintenance payments. Such arrangements can give rise to income tax and capital gains tax complications which may differ depending upon whether the recipient is a spouse or child. Where such a trust arrangement is created for a spouse, the payer will frequently have retained an interest in the settlement (he will generally be entitled to receive the income in excess of the maintenance payments and to have the trust assets returned to him when the maintenance ceases) and he would, under normal circumstances, be taxable on all the trust income. However, there is an exemption for this charge in s 660A of the Income and Corporation Taxes Act 1988 where the income arises under a settlement made to provide for a divorced or separated spouse.

9.11 One important tax consideration is that, whereas maintenance payments are normally tax-free in the hands of the recipient, any payment she receives from the trust will be taxable as her income. The payer will pay tax on any surplus income not distributed to the payee, but as he is not being taxed on the income earned by the trustees out of which the distributions are made he is, in effect, obtaining tax relief for the payments made. Whilst this may suit the payer, it could place the payee in a disadvantageous situation. It may be possible to circumvent this problem by using a trust in tandem with a maintenance agreement. The trust would act as a back-up arrangement under which payments would be made to the payee by the trustees only if the payer defaulted on his obligations under the maintenance agreement. As long as the payments continue under the maintenance order the normal rules will apply, but the payee has the security of knowing that the trust is there if payments cease.

9.12 The situation with regard to payments to children is somewhat different. Again, a secured maintenance arrangement may be a settlement but, under s 660B of the Income and Corporation Taxes Act 1988, income from the trust will be taxable as the father's income and not the child's. This puts them in the same position as they would be under a normal maintenance agreement whereby the payer receives no tax relief and receipts by the child are not taxed as the child's income. Secured maintenance payments also give rise to capital gains tax difficulties, as the transfer of the assets into the trust will be a deemed disposal by the settlor, the gain being calculated by reference to the market value of the assets at the date the settlement is created. Consideration could be given to transferring into the trust assets with a value which does not exceed the acquisition value by more than the amount of the relevant indexation allowance, or assets which are not chargeable to capital gains tax, for example sterling cash.

CAPITAL GAINS TAX

9.13 Following the Finance Act 1991 which introduced the provisions relating to the separate taxation of husband and wife, each spouse's gains and losses are computed separately, being taxed on the party concerned. Each spouse is entitled to a separate annual exemption, currently £7,500 in 2001/2002. Transfers can still be made between husband and wife on a 'no gain/no loss' basis whereby the recipient takes on the transferor's base cost which will apply for the purpose of calculating the gain on future disposals. This 'no gain/no loss' basis continues throughout the year of separation. Transfers after the end of the year of separation will give rise to capital gains tax in the normal way and will normally be deemed to take effect at market value.

9.14 Thus, where there is to be a transfer from one spouse to the other of an asset with a substantial inherent capital gain, an immediate tax charge can be avoided if the transfer is made before the end of the year of separation. However, the recipient spouse must take into account the transferor's base cost (or the value at 31 March 1982 if later) on any subsequent disposal and will, at that time, suffer the full capital gains charge unless the asset is held until death, when a tax-free uplift in value is applied. If the asset is likely to be disposed of before death, there may be occasions where the spouses would prefer the transfer of assets to take place in a year following the year of separation so that each party can bear the capital gains tax attributable to their respective periods of ownership.

9.15 The contingent capital gains tax on the disposal or transfer of assets should always be borne in mind and taken into account when valuing the resources available to the two spouses. Moreover, it must be noted that the Inland Revenue is not bound to accept the parties' or the court's assessment of the value of assets. It will be necessary, in calculating a capital gain where a disposal is not at arm's length, to arrive at the price which the assets might reasonably fetch in the open market. This may often be the subject of negotiation with the Inland Revenue.

The family home

9.16 The family home will, in most cases, be exempt from capital gains tax on the basis that it is the principal private residence (PPR). If there is more than one home, it is important to ascertain which is the couple's PPR. It is possible to make an election to determine which property will be the PPR, such an election having to be made within two years of the date on which such determination becomes necessary. Any property which is not a PPR will be subject to capital gains tax on transfer or disposal in the normal way. A husband and wife living together will be allowed only one PPR and it is important to consider how separation and divorce can affect this relief.

9.17 When a property has been a person's PPR throughout the entire period of ownership, the whole gain on disposal is exempt from tax. However, the last

36 months of ownership of a property that has at any time been a PPR is exempt in all cases. Thus, if the matrimonial home is to be sold or transferred by a party to the marriage who has left the matrimonial home, the disposal will be exempt from capital gains tax as long as it takes place within 36 months of the date of departure. If a property has been the individual's PPR for only part of the period of ownership, only a proportionate part of the gain is exempt. The last 36 months' ownership is also still fully exempt.

9.18 The Inland Revenue has also published an extra-statutory concession which alleviates the situation if a transfer to the other spouse takes place more than 36 months after it ceases to be the transferor's PPR. Under the concession the exemption will continue to apply as long as:

(a)   the matrimonial home remains the PPR of the other spouse; and
(b)   the disposer does not acquire another residence on which he claims PPR.

The concession is, therefore, of limited assistance as frequently the departing spouse will have acquired another residence and it enables the relief to apply only on a transfer of the property to the spouse who remains in residence and not on a disposal.

9.19 The position with regard to the family home can be further complicated when children are involved. In such cases, it may be ordered that the family house be held in joint names of the two spouses on trust for sale with the wife and children being allowed to continue to live in it for a specific period – such as until the youngest child reaches the age of 18 or ceases full-time education. At that time the property is sold and the proceeds divided between the two spouses. This sort of order is generally known as a *Mesher* order after the case of *Mesher v Mesher and Hall* [1980] 1 All ER 126 in which it was first used. These orders are not suitable to all circumstances as, whilst they may solve a short-term difficulty, there can be problems when the house comes to be sold and the wife's share may be insufficient to re-house her. If such an order is imposed, the capital gains tax position needs to be carefully considered, particularly in view of the fact that the arrangement may constitute a settlement.

EXTRACTING FUNDS FROM BUSINESS INTERESTS

9.20 For many individuals who own a family business, the major portion of their assets (apart from the family home) is tied into their businesses and, therefore, consideration needs to be given to ways of extracting funds from the business in a tax and commercially efficient manner (see also Chapter 7, 'Raising Funds for the Settlement'). In some situations, it is sufficient to boost the income of the payer of maintenance by the payment of dividends or increased remuneration. These payments may, of course, give rise to associated tax and, in the case of remuneration, National Insurance liabilities and may affect the cash flow of the business.

9.21 Apart from the need to enhance income, it is frequently necessary to raise a capital sum where the settlement of the divorce proceedings includes the payment of a capital sum. One possible method of raising capital from business assets is borrowing against the value of those assets, although interest on borrowing to pay a lump sum to a divorced spouse would not be eligible for income tax relief. Alternatively, if an individual has a loan account with his company he could take repayment of this tax-free. Should this cause cash flow difficulties for the company, he could consider obtaining bank borrowings to replace the funds withdrawn and, as long as certain conditions are fulfilled, the interest on the borrowings would be eligible for loan interest relief. Very broadly the conditions are:

(a)   the loan is to purchase ordinary shares or to make a loan to a close company;

(b)   the borrower is an individual who either:
    (i)   alone or with certain associates has a material interest (broadly, 5 per cent of ordinary share capital) in the company; or
    (ii) holds any ordinary shares and works for the greater part of his time in the management or conduct of the company or an associated company.

9.22 Those in partnership could consider a similar route by withdrawing their partnership capital (assuming this is not already financed by borrowings) and borrowing funds to inject into the partnership. Again, as long as certain conditions are met, the interest payments on the loan will be eligible for income tax relief. The conditions are:

(a)   the loan must be for the purchase of a share in or making an advance to a partnership;

(b)   the individual must be a member of the partnership but not a limited partner up to and including when the loan interest is paid;

(c)   where the advance is to the partnership the money must be used for the purposes of its trade, profession or vocation.

9.23 It should be borne in mind that the timing of capital withdrawals from a company or business can be of significance. Where borrowings are taken out either for a loan to a close company or to a partnership, any capital recoveries by the borrower after the loan has been applied will be treated as a reduction of the loan with a consequent reduction in tax relief. Borrowings will not be the solution in all cases and it may be necessary to resort to a disposal of business assets to raise cash and consideration should be given to whether any reliefs are available to mitigate the attendant tax liabilities. For instance, retirement relief may be due if the individual is disposing of business assets and has attained the age of 50 or is retiring below that age for reasons of ill health.

9.24 Retirement relief began to be phased out from 6 April 1999 and will no longer be available for disposals after 5 April 2003. A gradually reducing amount of relief is, however, available until then. The provisions are complex and are contained in s 163 and s 164 of and Sch 6 to the Taxation of Chargeable Gains Act 1992. Very broadly, the business assets to which the relief can apply must fall into one of the following categories:

(a) the whole or part of an unincorporated business including a partnership share – a disposal will qualify provided that, throughout a period of at least one year ending on the date of the disposal, the business or share has been owned by the individual making the disposal;

(b) assets used in a business which has ceased – the individual can obtain relief on a disposal of business assets sold within one year after the cessation;

(c) shares or securities of a company – to qualify, the company must be the individual's 'personal company' (ie one in which he can exercise at least 5 per cent of the voting rights), it must be a trading company or the holding company of a trading group and the individual must be a full-time working officer or employee of the company. Relief may be restricted if the company's assets are not all eligible business assets, for example if they include investments.

9.25 In addition, relief may be available for disposals of assets used in an office or employment, assets owned by a partner and used in a partnership business and for some trustee shareholdings or business assets. For disposals between 6 April 2000 and 5 April 2001 relief was available for the first £150,000 of gain plus half the gain between £150,000 and £600,000, ie a maximum of £375,000 was available on qualifying gains of £600,000 or more. For subsequent years, the levels of relief are as follows:

Disposals after	*100% relief*	*50% relief*	*Maximum*
5 April 2001	£100,000	£100,000–£400,000	£250,000
5 April 2002	£50,000	£50,000–£200,000	£125,000
5 April 2003	Nil	Nil	Nil

Full retirement relief is available only where all the necessary conditions have been satisfied throughout a qualifying period of at least 10 years. An appropriate percentage of the full relief is available where the qualifying period is at least one year but less than 10 years.

Taper relief

9.26 At the same time as providing for the phasing out of retirement relief, the Finance Act 1998 introduced a new form of relief known as taper relief for disposals after 5 April 1998. Taper relief reduces the chargeable gain according to the length of time an asset has been held and the reductions available for business assets are greater than those for non-business assets. The Finance Act 2000 increased the benefits of taper relief for disposals of business assets after 5 April 2000 and also widened the definition of business assets for these purposes.

Business assets

9.27 There are detailed provisions in the legislation determining qualification as a business asset and professional advice should be sought before reliance is placed on the availability of the relief. Broadly, however, business assets are either:

(a)   assets used by an individual for the purposes of a trade, partnership or by a 'qualifying company' (see below); or

(b)   shareholdings in a 'qualifying company' by reference to the individual.

9.28 The definition of 'qualifying company' has been amended in the Finance Act 2000 for periods of ownership after 5 April 2000, to include:

(a)   shareholdings of any size in unquoted trading companies;

(b)   shareholdings of any size held by employees or officers of quoted trading companies;

(c)   shareholdings of 5 per cent or more in quoted trading companies.

Prior to 5 April 2000 the definition was narrower, including only:

(a)   shareholdings of 25 per cent or more in trading companies (quoted or unquoted); or

(b)   shareholdings of 5 per cent or more in trading companies (quoted or unquoted) held by full-time working officers or employees.

9.29 For assets held prior to 5 April 2000, therefore, both sets of rules have to be applied to arrive at the correct rate of relief.

For disposals after 5 April 2000 of assets which have qualified as business assets since 5 April 1998, the following rates apply:

Years of ownership since 5/4/98	*Effective tax rate for higher rate taxpayer*
0	40%
1	35%
2	30%
3	20%
4	10%

Non-business assets

9.30 All other assets attract a less beneficial rate of relief, although there is a bonus deemed year of ownership for assets held on 17 March 1998. The rates applying are as follows:

Years of ownership since 5/4/98 (including bonus year)	Effective tax rate for higher rate taxpayer
0	40%
1	40%
2	40%
3	38%
4	36%
5	34%
6	32%
7	30%
8	28%
9	26%
10	24%

Mixed assets

9.31 Complex calculations will be required where an asset has been a business asset for only part of the period since 5 April 1998.

Clearly, there is a tax incentive to retain assets, particularly business assets, rather than to liquidate them early in order to fund a financial settlement.

Other considerations

9.32 A further method of reducing gains is by deducting excess trading losses that cannot be relieved against the individual's general income and the availability of such losses should, therefore, be borne in mind. The payer of a lump sum may also wish to consider borrowing from his company to meet his obligations under the divorce proceedings. Caution is, however, essential here as an individual may fall foul of provisions relating to loans to directors or participators of close companies which can give rise to advance corporation tax liabilities in the company. In addition, the individual could have a tax liability under the beneficial loan legislation if the loan is not made at a commercial rate of interest.

9.33 Rather than selling shares to a third party, consideration can be given to a company purchasing its own shares from the husband or the wife and subsequently cancelling them. This could be a course to be considered when a suitable purchaser cannot be identified, particularly one who would not be acceptable as a co-shareholder in the company. The Articles of Association must, however, permit the purchase by the company of its own shares.

9.34 Provisions enabling a company to purchase its own shares were introduced in the Companies Act 1981, prior to which such purchases were unlawful. However, the amendment of company law to permit a share buy-in did not ensure that there were no problems attaching to this type of transaction as, without special tax relief, the excess of the price paid for the shares over the capital originally subscribed would always be a distribution and effectively be treated as a dividend. This would result in the shareholder suffering higher rate taxes up to his marginal income tax rate.

9.35 Thus, special provisions were introduced in the Finance Act 1982 which ensure that, if certain conditions are satisfied, the payment by a company for its own shares will attract only a capital gains tax liability in the hands of the vendor. These special rules apply only if certain conditions are met. The principal conditions are:

(a)   the company must be unquoted;
(b)   the company must be either a trading company or the holding company of a trading group;
(c)   the purchase of the shares must be wholly or mainly to benefit the company's trade (or that of a 75 per cent subsidiary);
(d)   it must not be for a tax-avoidance motive;
(e)   the vendor must meet certain requirements as to residence and period of ownership; and
(f)   the vendor's shareholding must be eliminated or substantially redeemed, ie the proportion of the company's issued share capital held by him immediately after the purchase must not exceed 75 per cent of that held immediately before the purchase.

9.36 If the conditions are not met the funds received from the company will be treated as income rather than capital gains. At the present time, when the top rate of income tax and capital gains tax are the same, there may be little advantage in one route over the other.

9.37 It is possible that the settlement of the divorce proceedings may require the transfer of shares in one spouse's business to the other. Whereas transfers of business assets for no consideration may be eligible for holdover relief, it is doubtful that this relief will be helpful in most matrimonial situations as:

–   the recipient would have a reduced base cost in the event of a subsequent disposal; and
–   the relief is not available where there is actual consideration equal to the market value of the asset transferred. The Inland Revenue takes the view that the relinquishing of financial claims in exchange for the asset transferred can amount to actual consideration for this purpose.

INHERITANCE TAX

9.38 Transfers between spouses who are both domiciled in the UK are totally exempt from inheritance tax. The date of separation, which is the important date for looking at the income tax and capital gains tax consequences of a marriage breakdown, has no significance for inheritance tax purposes and the inter-spouse exemption continues until decree absolute so that property can be transferred up to that time free of all inheritance tax.

9.39 If, however, property is transferred after the date of the decree absolute there are other relieving provisions which may exempt the transfer from tax. Section 10 of the Inheritance Tax Act 1984 provides that a disposition will not be a transfer of value if it is not intended to confer gratuitous benefit and is made at arm's length between unconnected persons. The Senior Registrar of the Family Division has issued a statement with the Inland Revenue's agreement that this exemption will normally cover transfers of property pursuant to orders of the divorce court. The statement applies only to transfers made under court orders and the Inland Revenue may show more interest in consent orders than in contested orders. The exemption may apply to children as well as former spouses.

9.40 Section 11(1) of the Inheritance Tax Act 1984 provides that a disposition is not a transfer of value if it is made by one party to a marriage to the other party or to their child, if it is for the maintenance of the other spouse or for the maintenance, education or training of the child under age 18 or until full-time education ceases if later. Failing the availability of any of these exemptions, a transfer may be a potentially exempt transfer, if it is made directly to an individual or to a trust in which an individual has an interest in possession or to an accumulation and maintenance trust. The transfer will become fully exempt if the transferor survives the transfer by at least seven years.

OVERSEAS CONSIDERATIONS

9.41 Where there are substantial assets held in non-UK trusts or companies and one or both spouses are resident or domiciled overseas, careful consideration should be given to the possibility of structuring a settlement in a tax-efficient way. The issues are complex and specific specialist professional advice should be taken.

SHARE OPTIONS AND SHARE INCENTIVE SCHEMES

9.42 It is becoming increasingly common for key employees to receive share options or other share-based incentives as part of their reward, particularly in the fast-growing technology sector. There can be complex tax implications attaching to the exercise of options, depending upon the type of option scheme through which they are granted. This has become more complex now that the Inland Revenue have announced that it has become legal to pass on the employer's social security cost to the employees, by agreement. Many employees may be facing not only a 40 per cent income tax charge but an additional effective 7.14 per cent social security charge on the exercise of unapproved share options.

APPENDIX

Matrimonial Causes Act 1973, ss 25–25D

25   Matters to which court is to have regard in deciding how to exercise its powers under ss 23, 24 and 24A

(1) It shall be the duty of the court in deciding whether to exercise its powers under section 23, 24, 24A or 24B above and, if so, in what manner, to have regard to all the circumstances of the case, first consideration being given to the welfare while a minor of any child of the family who has not attained the age of eighteen.

(2) As regards the exercise of the powers of the court under section 23(1)(a), (b) or (c), 24, 24A or 24B above in relation to a party to the marriage, the court shall in particular have regard to the following matters –

    (a) the income, earning capacity, property and other financial resources which each of the parties to the marriage has or is likely to have in the foreseeable future, including in the case of earning capacity any increase in that capacity which it would in the opinion of the court be reasonable to expect a party to the marriage to take steps to acquire;

    (b) the financial needs, obligations and responsibilities which each of the parties to the marriage has or is likely to have in the foreseeable future;

    (c) the standard of living enjoyed by the family before the breakdown of the marriage;

    (d) the age of each party to the marriage and the duration of the marriage;

    (e) any physical or mental disability of either of the parties to the marriage;

    (f) the contributions which each of the parties has made or is likely in the foreseeable future to make to the welfare of the family, including any contribution by looking after the home or caring for the family;

    (g) the conduct of each of the parties, if that conduct is such that it would in the opinion of the court be inequitable to disregard it;

    (h) in the case of proceedings for divorce or nullity of marriage, the value to each of the parties to the marriage of any benefit which, by reason of the dissolution or annulment of the marriage, that party will lose the chance of acquiring.

(3) As regards the exercise of the powers of the court under section 23(1)(d), (e) or (f), (2) or (4), 24 or 24A above in relation to a child of the family, the court shall in particular have regard to the following matters –

    (a) the financial needs of the child;

    (b) the income, earning capacity (if any), property and other financial resources of the child;

(c) any physical or mental disability of the child;
(d) the manner in which he was being and in which the parties to the marriage expected him to be educated or trained;
(e) the considerations mentioned in relation to the parties to the marriage in paragraphs (a), (b), (c) and (e) of subsection (2) above.

(4) As regards the exercise of the powers of the court under section 23(1)(d), (e) or (f), (2) or (4), 24 or 24A above against a party to a marriage in favour of a child of the family who is not the child of that party, the court shall also have regard –

(a) to whether that party assumed any responsibility for the child's maintenance, and, if so, to the extent to which, and the basis upon which, that party assumed such responsibility and to the length of time for which that party discharged such responsibility;
(b) to whether in assuming and discharging such responsibility that party did so knowing that the child was not his or her own;
(c) to the liability of any other person to maintain the child.

25A Exercise of court's powers in favour of party to marriage on decree of divorce or nullity of marriage

(1) Where on or after the grant of a decree of divorce or nullity of marriage the court decides to exercise its powers under section 23(1)(a), (b) or (c), 24, 24A or 24B above in favour of a party to the marriage, it shall be the duty of the court to consider whether it would be appropriate so to exercise those powers that the financial obligations of each party towards the other will be terminated as soon after the grant of the decree as the court considers just and reasonable.

(2) Where the court decides in such a case to make a periodical payments or secured periodical payments order in favour of a party to the marriage, the court shall in particular consider whether it would be appropriate to require those payments to be made or secured only for such term as would in the opinion of the court be sufficient to enable the party in whose favour the order is made to adjust without undue hardship to the termination of his or her financial dependence on the other party.

(3) Where on or after the grant of a decree of divorce or nullity of marriage an application is made by a party to the marriage for a periodical payments or secured periodical payments order in his or her favour, then, if the court considers that no continuing obligation should be imposed on either party to make or secure periodical payments in favour of the other, the court may dismiss the application with a direction that the applicant shall not be entitled to make any future application in relation to that marriage for an order under section 23(1)(a) or (b) above.

25B Pensions

(1) The matters to which the court is to have regard under section 25(2) above include –

(a) in the case of paragraph (a), any benefits under a pension arrangement which a party to the marriage has or is likely to have, and

(b) in the case of paragraph (h), any benefits under a pension arrangement which, by reason of the dissolution or annulment of the marriage, a party to the marriage will lose the chance of acquiring,

and, accordingly, in relation to benefits under a pension arrangement, section 25(2)(a) above shall have effect as if 'in the foreseeable future' were omitted.

(2) ...

(3) The following provisions apply where, having regard to any benefits under a pension arrangement, the court determines to make an order under section 23 above.

(4) To the extent to which the order is made having regard to any benefits under a pension arrangement, the order may require the person responsible for the pension arrangement in question, if at any time any payment in respect of any benefits under the arrangement becomes due to the party with pension rights, to make a payment for the benefit of the other party.

(5) The order must express the amount of any payment required to be made by virtue of subsection (4) above as a percentage of the payment which becomes due to the party with pension rights.

(6) Any such payment by the person responsible for the arrangement –

(a) shall discharge so much of his liability to the party with pension rights as corresponds to the amount of the payment, and

(b) shall be treated for all purposes as a payment made by the party with pension rights in or towards the discharge of his liability under the order.

(7) Where the party with pension rights has a right of commutation under the arrangement, the order may require him to exercise it to any extent; and this section applies to any payment due in consequence of commutation in pursuance of the order as it applies to other payments in respect of benefits under the arrangement.

(7A) The power conferred by subsection (7) above may not be exercised for the purpose of commuting a benefit payable to the party with pension rights to a benefit payable to the other party.

(7B) The power conferred by subsection (4) or (7) above may not be exercised in relation to a pension arrangement which –

(a) is the subject of a pension sharing order in relation to the marriage, or

(b) has been the subject of pension sharing between the parties to the marriage.

(7C) In subsection (1) above, references to benefits under a pension arrangement include any benefits by way of pension, whether under a pension arrangement or not.

25C Pensions: lump sums

(1) The power of the court under section 23 above to order a party to a marriage to pay a lump sum to the other party includes, where the benefits which the party with pension rights has or is likely to have under a pension arrangement include any lump sum payable in respect of his death, power to make any of the following provision by the order.

(2) The court may –

(a) if the person responsible for the pension arrangement in question has power to determine the person to whom the sum, or any part of it, is to be paid, require him to pay the whole or part of that sum, when it becomes due, to the other party,
(b) if the party with pension rights has power to nominate the person to whom the sum, or any part of it, is to be paid, require the party with pension rights to nominate the other party in respect of the whole or part of that sum,
(c) in any other case, require the person responsible for the pension arrangement in question to pay the whole or part of that sum, when it becomes due, for the benefit of the other party instead of to the person to whom, apart from the order, it would be paid.

(3) Any payment by the person responsible for the arrangement under an order made under section 23 above by virtue of this section shall discharge so much of his liability in respect of the party with pension rights as corresponds to the amount of the payment.

(4) The powers conferred by this section may not be exercised in relation to a pension arrangement which –

(a) is the subject of a pension sharing order in relation to the marriage, or
(b) has been the subject of pension sharing between the parties to the marriage.

25D Pensions: supplementary

(1) Where –

(a) an order made under section 23 above by virtue of section 25B or 25C above imposes any requirement on the person responsible for a pension arrangement ('the first arrangement') and the party with pension rights acquires rights under another pension arrangement ('the new arrangement') which are derived (directly or indirectly) from the whole of his rights under the first arrangement, and

(b) the person responsible for the new arrangement has been given notice in accordance with regulations made by the Lord Chancellor,

the order shall have effect as if it has been made instead in respect of the person responsible for the new arrangement.

(2) The Lord Chancellor may by regulations –

(a) in relation to any provision of sections 25B or 25C above which authorises the court making an order under section 23 above to require the person responsible for a pension arrangement to make a payment for the benefit of the other party, make provision as to the person to whom, and the terms on which, the payment is to be made,

(ab) make, in relation to payment under a mistaken belief as to the continuation in force of a provision included by virtue of section 25B or 25C above in an order under section 23 above, provision about the rights or liabilities of the payer, the payee or the person to whom the payment was due,

(b) require notices to be given in respect of changes of circumstances relevant to such orders which include provision made by virtue of sections 25B and 25C above,

(ba) make provision for the person responsible for a pension arrangement to be discharged in prescribed circumstances from a requirement imposed by virtue of section 25B or 25C above,

(c), (d) . . .

(e) make provision about calculation and verification in relation to the valuation of –

(i)   benefits under a pension arrangement, or

(ii)   shareable state scheme rights,

for the purposes of the court's functions in connection with the exercise of any of its powers under this Part of this Act.

. . .

(2A) Regulations under subsection (2) (e) above may include –

(a) provision for calculation or verification in accordance with guidance from time to time prepared by a prescribed person, and

(b) provision by reference to regulations under section 30 or 49 of the Welfare Reform and Pensions Act 1999.

(2B) Regulations under subsection (2) above may make different provision for different cases.

(2C) Power to make regulations under this section shall be exercisable by statutory instrument which shall be subject to annulment in pursuance of a resolution of either House of Parliament.

(3) In this section and sections 25B and 25C above –

'occupational pension scheme' has the same meaning as in the Pension Schemes Act 1993;

'the party with pension rights' means the party to the marriage who has or is likely to have benefits under a pension arrangement and 'the other party' means the other party to the marriage;

'pension arrangement' means –

    (a) an occupational pension scheme,

    (b) a personal pension scheme,

    (c) a retirement annuity contract,

    (d) an annuity or insurance policy purchased, or transferred, for the purpose of giving effect to rights under an occupational pension scheme or a personal pension scheme, and

    (e) an annuity purchased, or entered into, for the purpose of discharging liability in respect of a pension credit under section 29(1)(b) of the Welfare Reform and Pensions Act 1999 or under corresponding Northern Ireland legislation;

'personal pension scheme' has the same meaning as in the Pension Schemes Act 1993;

'prescribed' means prescribed by regulations;

'retirement annuity contract' means a contract or scheme approved under Chapter III of Part XIV of the Income and Corporation Taxes Act 1988;

'shareable state scheme rights' has the same meaning as in section 21A(1) above; and

'trustees or managers', in relation to an occupational pension scheme or a personal pension scheme, means –

    (a) in the case of a scheme established under a trust, the trustees of the scheme, and

    (b) in any other case, the managers of the scheme.

(4) In this section and sections 25B and 25C above, references to the person responsible for a pension arrangement are –

    (a) in the case of an occupational pension scheme or a personal pension scheme, to the trustees or managers of the scheme,

    (b) in the case of a retirement annuity contract or an annuity falling within paragraph (d) or (e) of the definition of 'pension arrangement' above, the provider of the annuity, and

    (c) in the case of an insurance policy falling within paragraph (d) of the definition of that expression, the insurer.

SFLA Good Practice in Family Law on Disclosure

1. Introduction

Non disclosure or misleading disclosure and a belief in the other's non disclosure are the primary factors in the high costs, delays and dissatisfaction with ancillary relief resolution on divorce. When there is full disclosure, the potential uncertainty caused by our highly discretionary-based resolution system should not alone cause such costs, delay or dissatisfaction: two experienced family law solicitors, with counsel as necessary and with clients accepting advice, should in most cases be able to resolve a matter without needing to go to court.

With costs of obtaining disclosure often high, and clients sometimes not confident that the legal system will achieve full disclosure, some clients are engaging in self-help steps to obtain disclosure. Whilst some actions are not illegal or unlawful, such measures inevitably inflame the situation and often make settlement less likely.

Further, the obtaining and giving of disclosure process can allow the parties a legal process to express their bitterness, frustration and animosities arising out of the relationship and its breakdown. The forum of the divorce suit and, now, the children arrangements are not so available thus it finds another but expensive outlet. Often the conduct of giving/obtaining disclosure is the last remaining battleground.

The Good Practice Committee is anxious to remove these opportunities for such emotional battles. In part, it can be achieved by a change in court procedure, and the SFLA supports the Ancillary Relief Rules Working Party recommendations. In part, it can be achieved by strong judicial guidance eg remarks on conduct of cases and preparation by Thorpe J in F v F [1995] 2 FLR 45 and by Wilson J in T v T referred to at para 6. However, it can also be achieved through good practice of SFLA members, who represent a significant proportion of parties in divorce proceedings. This paper sets out to help and guide members. Inevitably, as set out at the end, members have a duty to follow client's instructions, or cease acting provided the client knew at the outset that the solicitor would work in accordance with the Code of Practice. But solicitors often underestimate their power of persuasion and influence over clients. Many clients can be persuaded by good reason to follow good practice rather than give misleading disclosure or undertake unnecessary investigation. This is the duty upon SFLA members. It is possible to improve radically the conduct of ancillary relief matters in respect of disclosure.

Application of the Code of Practice cannot be in isolation from the law, judicial recommended practice or The Guide to Professional Conduct of Solicitors. This Guidance therefore deals with a summary of the law as well as our recommendations of good practice.

2.   The Duty to Disclose

The specific obligation depends on the proceedings. It must also be remembered that disclosure relates to both facts and documents.

2.1   Divorce and Similar Petitions

RSC Order 24 r 1 applies to a defended cause begun by Petition. It provides that after the close of pleadings in an action there shall be discovery by the parties of the documents which are or have been in their possession, custody or power relating to matters in question in the action.

2.2   Finances Ancillary to Divorce

Each party owes a duty to the Court to give full and frank disclosure in ancillary relief applications: Practice Direction (Case Management) of 31 January 1995 [1995] 1 All ER 586 and for example Livesey v Jenkins [1985] 1 All ER. Anything less may render it impossible for the Court to carry out its balancing exercise eg as required under section 25 MCA, perhaps invalidating any Order made and making adverse costs a real likelihood, including against legal representatives.

2.3   Children Act Proceedings

There are specific requirements. Local authorities in care proceedings have a 'high duty in law to be open in disclosure of all relevant materials affecting' the welfare of the child: R v Hants CC Ex p K [1990] 1 FLR 330. See also Oxfordshire CC v M [1994] 1 FLR 175. Equally when the child's best interests demand it, there is immunity from disclosure: see David Burrows' article at (1995) Sol Jo 60. But see particularly para 4 of the Practice Direction (Case Management) set out at para 2.2. See also SFLA guidance on 'Good Practice when acting for Children'.

2.4   Generally in Civil Proceedings

'But nowadays the general rule is that, whilst a party is entitled to privacy in seeking out the cards for his hand, once he has put his hand together, the litigation is to be conducted with all the cards face up on the table. Furthermore, most of the cards have to be put down well before the hearing.' Naylor v Preston Area Health Authority [1987] 2 All ER 353, per Donaldson MR at 360.

2.5   Judicial Involvement

There is a clear trend for more judicial involvement in the conduct of family law cases including the seeking and giving of disclosure. This has been made very clear from the Practice Direction set out in 2.2. Moreover in F v F [1995] 2 FLR 45 at 70A Thorpe J said that 'ancillary relief applications in the Family Division are not purely adversarial. The court has an independent duty to discharge the function imposed by statute. The court has from that duty the power to investigate and the power to ensure compliance with the duty of full and frank disclosure owed by litigants'. There is no doubt that similar sentiments would apply in children cases.

Good Practice

1.   Disclosure is of such vital importance to the court as the means to produce a just outcome that in giving disclosure, parties and their legal advisers should err on the side of too much rather than too little.

2.   Para 1.7 of the SFLA Code of Practice reads: 'The solicitor should aim to avoid mistrust between the parties by encouraging at an early stage full, frank and clear disclosure of information and openness in dealings'.

3.   Whilst certain information, eg s 25(2) MCA, must be given, we believe the duty to disclose extends to any fact within a party's knowledge which might materially affect the exercise of the court's discretion or powers.

3.   The Importance that the Court Attaches to the Duty of Disclosure in Financial Cases

The courts regard failure to disclose as a reprehensible act. It may be occasionally regarded as 'conduct', may give rise to an inference of greater assets and/or lead to costs penalties against a party and possibly against a legal representative.

'I appreciate that it has been held that a spouse's behaviour in the ancillary litigation, specifically a dishonest failure to make full disclosure, amounts to [relevant s 25(2)] conduct: Desai v Desai (1983) Family Law 46 and B v B [1988] 2 FLR 490. But I agree with Thorpe J in P v P [1994] 2 FLR 381 at p 306A–C that a dishonest disclosure will more appropriately be reflected in the inference that the resources are larger than have been disclosed, in which case it will fall within s 25(2)(a) and/or in the order for costs ...': per Wilson J in T v T [1994] 2 FLR 1083.

This approach was taken in E v E [1990] 2 FLR 233 where a husband's failure to disclose information about Swiss bank accounts and land necessitated an expensive and rigorous investigation into his affairs. He was ordered to pay the costs of both sides for the investigation. Ewbank J also held that the husband's failure to disclose justified any inferences which were proper to be drawn against him.

Good Practice

There is at least a good practice duty (and probably a duty in law) to tell clients of the obligation to give full disclosure, the severity of the court's approach to non or misleading disclosure, and the adverse inferences that are likely to be made and the likely costs sanctions. It is almost certainly negligent not to tell clients.

4. The Timing of On-going Disclosure

4.1   Rule 2.58 FPR requires the Affidavit in support of the application for Financial Relief to contain full particulars of the Applicant's property and income and to state the facts relied on in support of the application. In children cases, Rule 4.17 FPR prohibits reliance on evidence if a written statement of the substance of oral evidence has not been filed and copy documents produced by the time laid down by the Court (and in default before the hearing).

4.2   The courts have clearly expected there to be an obligation to disclose developments on an ongoing basis. Livesey v Jenkins (2.2 above) for example decided that there was an obligation on the wife to disclose her engagement immediately.

4.3   The documents and information that must be volunteered on an ongoing basis during the litigation are those which add materially to the overall picture, or alter disclosure already given, or are such as might reasonably affect the negotiating position.

4.4   The duty to disclose and, by extension, to update that disclosure, is policed by penalising the person who fails to do so by a costs order or adverse inferences.

4.5   Producing information, including updating or varying disclosure, at the last moment often leads to an adjournment and/or a penalty on costs. This may be against the solicitors.

Good Practice

1.   Disclosure should be given as early as possible, to avoid mistrust, to save costs and to expedite consideration of terms of settlement.

2.   After any disclosure, there is a good practice obligation, irrespective of any obligation in law, to advise the client to notify any material changes in that disclosure, as soon as practicable.

3.   In children's cases, we believe there is an even greater and expeditious duty to disclose any changes where they are or may be material to any arrangements concerning a child or his/her best interests.

4.   It is (at least) good practice always to advise the client to up-date the disclosure given by the client (even if to say that the circumstances remain the same) prior to trial. The timing of that update is defined by two factors: – as late as possible to ensure that there is only minimum change between the date of the up-dating and the date of the trial; – and as early as will ensure that there is an opportunity to avoid the costs of the litigation through achieving a negotiated settlement.

5.   Privilege and Disclosure

Privileged communications are generally protected from disclosure in evidence in any civil proceedings. The law of privilege is complex but solicitor/client privilege covers communications between a party and his/her legal advisers and with third parties in the preparation and conduct of the case and regarding the litigation.

There is also the privilege that attaches in specific defined instances to correspondence and discussions between the parties and their advisers regarding compromise of any litigation etc. Quite different legal principles can apply to these two forms of privilege.

There are however statutory exceptions. In children's cases, privilege can be overridden by the best interests of the child: see Oxfordshire County Council v M [1994] 1 FLR 175 and David Burrows' articles at [1995] Fam Law 37 and (1995) Sol Jo 60. See also Law Society guidance in the context of child abuse and abduction: Annex 16B, Guide to Professional Conduct (6th Edition).

Simply marking a letter as 'without prejudice' or 'without prejudice save as to costs' does not thereby protect factual disclosure from being properly treated as open.

Good Practice

1.   Facts should not be disclosed in without prejudice correspondence. There should be an open letter containing the disclosed information and a separate letter making any privileged proposals.

2.   A solicitor may refuse to accept any factual information given in another solicitor's privileged letter. The writer of the letter should be invited to repeat it in an open letter or show good reason why it should not be treated as open. If he/she refuses, the recipient could treat that part as open, thereafter referring

to it in open correspondence and/or if necessary have the issue adjudicated at an interlocutory hearing.

3.   Great care must be exercised in using privilege correctly.

4.   The issue of privilege and confidentiality is a complex one of law, procedure and ethics. If in any doubt, the solicitor should forthwith consult the Law Society Ethics Department (0171 242 1222) as to the ethical position and the Law Society Professional Adviser (0171 320 5172) as to the professional position.

5.   The opportunity of privileged communications between parties to litigation is a tremendous resource in the English legal system to encourage maximum attempts to settle and should be fully utilised by solicitors on behalf of clients. Furthermore, although there is no duty to negotiate per se but only to put forward a good offer of settlement (Wilson J at [1994] Fam Law 504), the SFLA member will also take account of the wider advantages to the client and family of a settlement, and avoiding a contested hearing, in considering any offers, negotiations and compromises.

6.   The Legal Limitations to Self-Help in Obtaining Disclosure

The Good Practice Committee is very aware of the real ethical difficulties faced by clients and solicitors when the prospect arises of self-help in obtaining disclosure. There is still largely an adversarial process. The reality is that some people specifically hide assets and/or make obtaining disclosure difficult and costly. Justice cannot be done without a significant degree of disclosure. We do not condemn self-help where it can be justified (see below). Further we recognise that there are exceptional cases where it is the only route, or certainly by far the quickest/cheapest route, to obtain satsifactory disclosure. Equally, we are conscious that such self-help is fraught with problems. Even if actions that a client or solicitor contemplates are lawful, there is a good practice duty on a solicitor to advise the client to consider the consequences including:

   – more likely to create a war zone mentality with similar, vindictive and corresponding action by the other party
   – likely to increase costs
   – have an adverse effect on children
   – may result in an order for costs if the self-help is shown to be unjustified or unreasonable
   – may either make settlement more likely or much less likely
   – but may obtain disclosure that would otherwise stay hidden.

6.1   When Can Self-Help be Justified?

Wilson J at [1994] Fam Law 506 said: 'We would extend this beyond simple photocopying to other lawful action without force. But the burden of showing the justification is wholly on the person taking the action and it is a relatively heavy one, proportionate to the severity of self-help action taken.

My feeling is that if the wife gives an account of her husband, which includes any past financial dishonesty, whether to herself or to a third party, or accounts any threat or statement by him such as reasonably leads to the conclusion that he is not likely within the divorce proceedings to give a full account of his financial position, it is permissible to advise her to take photocopies of such documents as she can obtain without the use of force.'

6.2 What Action Can be Justified?

It is inappropriate to give a list. But in T v T [1994] 2 FLR 1083, Wilson J did not condemn taking photocopies of such of the husband's documents that she could locate without force and by scouring the dustbin. He did condemn using force to obtain documents.

6.3 The Timing of the Return of Documents

Wilson J said at [1994] Fam Law 506 that his view was that (justifiably taken) copies 'are discoverable documents which should logically be disclosed at, but only at, discovery stage or earlier if the husband's solicitor so requests. In other words, they can, absent such a request, be withheld until after the husband has sworn his affidavit of means and until the wife's questionnaire is served.' In T v T (above), he said the wife's conduct in failing to reveal her possession of original and copy documents until late in the proceedings was unacceptable.

Good Practice

1.   In respect of any of his comments in T v T which were obiter, rather than ratio, we support what Wilson J said. We also support his comments made on the subject in his article at [1994] Fam Law 504. We welcome such judicial guidance and initiative in tackling this difficult subject.

2.   Self-help where physical damage is done is potentially dangerous, given that there may be issues of criminal damage or other offences, which may move the difficult family litigation into the entirely new and more charged forum of police involvement and perhaps the Criminal Courts.

3.   Solicitors should remember that the court has extreme powers eg Anton Piller Orders, to investigate where non-disclosure is likely.

4.   Solicitors and clients must beware of the excitement and drama engendered by some self-help which can cause a loss of objectivity and of professional judgment and an overlooking of the intended end result. It can also result in solicitors overlooking the several complex issues of professional conduct that arise in this area.

7.   Reading Misdirected Privileged Mail and Other Privileged Documents

Principle 16.07 of the Law Society's Guide to Professional Conduct and accompanying commentaries sets out the position at present adopted by the Law Society. We will not conceal that we have found the Principle and commentaries difficult to understand, to reconcile and to apply to normal practice in family law. But two different situations arise; first, the client obtains privileged letters etc passing between the other spouse etc and his/her solicitor and intends showing to the client's solicitor, and secondly, privileged documents, letters eg between solicitor and client are mistakenly sent to the other solicitor.

7.1   Clients Obtaining Privileged Communications

Where a client tells a solicitor that he has obtained solicitor/client privileged documents, letters etc belonging to his spouse, the solicitor should say to the client that he does not want to know about the document, contents etc and, further, should tell the client not to read it and instead to replace it, destroy it if it was only a copy, or send it to the solicitor to forward on unread. Acting in this way would avoid the solicitor in any conflict with the professional obligation to act in the best interests of the client.

Where a solicitor receives a letter from his client and knows from reading the covering letter that what he has received is privileged, the solicitor should not, following commentary 4 to Principle 16.07, read the attachments but should forthwith return them to the client or, preferably, should recommend to the client that the solicitor should forthwith return them direct to the other solicitor.

In any event, the client should be recommended to disclose via the solicitor at the earliest opportunity that the client has, and has read, privileged documents. The other solicitor should be told what the client and/or the solicitor has read and what notes have been taken.

A conflict between solicitor and client only arises if the solicitor reads privileged documents and the client does not or does not know the contents. It does not arise if the client reads and the solicitor does not know the contents.

See also the Ablitt case (7.2 below) about the solicitor not continuing to act when he has read privileged documents.

7.2   Privileged Letters etc Wrongly Sent to Other Solicitor

Where a solicitor is sent a document by mistake from the other side, then although the solicitor could not be said to have sought to obtain access (see commentary 4 to Principle 16.07), nevertheless he should not read the letter or document if he is to comply with commentary 5 to Principle 16.07. If a solicitor knows immediately ie within the first few sentences of a letter, that it was sent to him by mistake, then he should stop reading. If he were to act in this way, then he would have nothing to seek instructions upon, need not tell his client and this would avoid a dilemma. Further, we are led to believe by the Law Society that a solicitor would not thereby be professionally criticised although each case depends on its own facts.

But if the solicitor reads a material part of the documents etc and then realises that it was not meant for him but has to concede that the information already read could be very useful to his client, then he is under a duty to discuss the pros and cons with his client. In particular, he should mention that he will have to notify forthwith the other side that he has received this document by mistake and explain to his client the likelihood of the other side obtaining an injunction concerning the document and the costs implications, and/or the case being more likely to go to court.

Further, in Ablitt v Mills and Reeve (1995) The Times 25 October, Mr Justice Blackburne gave an injunction restraining solicitors from continuing to act for a party in civil litigation where the solicitors mistakenly received privileged documents sent to them by the other side's counsel's clerk and which on direct client instructions they had read. The judge said it offended elementary notions of justice if one party, having knowingly taken advantage of such a mistake, could nevertheless continue to have the services of advisers who now had an accurate view of the other side's adviser's views on merits etc.

Good Practice

1.   In the context of family cases, confidential (but disclosable) and privileged (non-disclosable) documents are often stored together by parties. Whereas there might be justification for seizing and obtaining the former, a client has to be advised and warned, in the starkest and dire of terms, of the strong professional and judicial condemnation of obtaining and reading the latter ie solicitor/client privileged papers. Clients should be discouraged from actions that might lead to seeing privileged documents.

2.   We recommend the following r 2.63 question where it is thought relevant: 'Does the [Petitioner] have in his possession, power or control any personal and/or privileged papers or documents belonging to the Respondent? If so, he is required to produce them forthwith and in the case of privileged papers, to state if he and his legal advisers have retained any originals, copies or notes thereon and if so, to deliver them up forthwith. Please explain when and the exact circumstances in which these personal and/or privileged papers came into his possession. This request is a continuing one until trial'.

3.   A solicitor has a good practice duty to recommend to the client to disclose forthwith to the other party's solicitor when the client has privileged papers belonging to another party. SFLA members must have confidence that fellow members will give suitable recommendations/advice to their clients where

privileged communications are concerned. The most obvious exceptions are where certain criminal or civil offences eg child abduction/abuse are thereby disclosed or a child's best interests clearly outweigh the importance of privilege.

4. It is at least good practice, when handing back privileged papers on instructions, to say the extent to which the solicitor has read them and confirm no copies or notes have been kept.

5. It is good practice management to take steps to minimise the risk of correspondence going astray. One example is the use of window envelopes.

6. Given that many parties in family law litigation still live together, the opportunities for solicitor/client correspondence being obtained by the other party are quite high. Where solicitor's letters are sent, and kept, should be considered at the outset between solicitor and client.

7. Where a solicitor does read privileged documents, he must now consider whether he should withdraw from the case following the Ablitt decision (above). Even if it is felt that there is no legal duty to do so, it is important to take account of the perception of the other party and the fact of the solicitor's continuance in the case may make a settlement less likely and the other party more resolved to go to the final hearing. However the extra costs of changing solicitors must also be considered.

8. Intercepting Mail

In a jointly occupied property, there are often many opportunities to intercept post within the home. Opening another's post and not giving back either as soon as possible or after immediate copying is deprecated by the courts and may result in at least a sanction on costs (T v T above). Opening the post and giving back as soon as possible may still be deprecated by the courts and would need to have good justification.

In respect of intercepting mail, the relevant statute is the Post Office Act 1953 section 55. It is a criminal offence to fraudulently retain, secrete, keep or detain any postal packet which is in the course of transmission by post. The course of transmission is from the time of its being delivered to any post box or office to the time of its being delivered to the premises of the addressee.

Good Practice

If clients ask about the possibility of taking these steps, there is a good practice duty to advise the client about: (1) the court's sanctions if the court should subsequently find there was not the necessary justification; (2) the inevitable antagonism and friction that will be created (when discovered), thereby making settlement less likely; (3) the inevitable opportunity to obtain disclosure (more quickly or at less cost) if justification exists to believe full disclosure will not be, or has not been, given.

9.   Telephone Tapping/Interceptions

It is a criminal offence (Interception of Communications Act 1985 Section 1) intentionally to intercept a communication in the course of its transmission by post or other telecommunications, without reasonable grounds for believing there was consent to do so. The position of what is interception is unclear.

As regards taping telephone conversations between solicitors, the commentary to Principle 20.01 of the Guide to Professional Conduct states that the other solicitor should normally be warned that the conversation is going to be recorded. However this warning may be dispensed with in cases where the solicitor believes that considerations of courtesy are outweighed by other factors.

Good Practice

1.   It is probably not wrong for a spouse to record a telephone conversation in which he/she is taking part or on a telephone in a jointly occupied property. If intending to use taped calls, clients should be advised that courts rarely find such evidence attractive, especially in children's cases. Courts are often highly critical of parties who introduce telephoning taping evidence. Doing so is also likely to inflame a situation.

2.   If clients ask about the possibility of taking such steps, there is a good practice duty to advise the client about: (1) the court's sanctions if the court should subsequently find there was not the necessary justification; (2) the inevitable antagonism and friction that will be created (when discovered), thereby making settlement less likely; (3) the inevitable opportunity to obtain disclosure (more quickly or at less cost) if justification exists to believe full disclosure will not be, or has not been, given.

3.   Save in very exceptional circumstances, which the solicitor must be able to justify to a high standard, a solicitor in a family law case should not secretly tape a telephone conversation with another solicitor.

10.   Entrapment

In this context of investigation and disclosure, entrapment is chiefly where a question is asked to which an answer is already known but which is intended to test truthfulness of the person giving the answer. Hildebrand v Hildebrand

[1992] 1 FLR 244 concerned an application by the husband to require the wife to answer a questionnaire to which she objected on the basis that the husband had by self-help obtained documents which enabled him to know and reveal the truthfulness or otherwise of answers to some of the questions.

The High Court held that the essence of the questionnaire procedure (and by extension, the discovery process) was a genuine enquiry in ignorance of true and complete facts. Where the requested documents or answers were already held/known, it would be oppressive to order replies.

Good Practice

We set out an example of good practice in balancing entrapment and obtaining disclosure. If a wife has a statement in her possession of a bank account in her husband's name at, say, Lloyds Bank yet the husband has failed to disclose this bank account in his affidavit, and perhaps in a reply to questionnaire:

(1) it is not good practice simply to ask if he has any more bank accounts;

(2) it is clearly good practice to ask if there are any more bank accounts stating that the wife knows of the specific Lloyds account;

(3) it is also good practice to ask if there are any more bank accounts and state that the wife has in her possession documentary details of at least one hitherto undisclosed account.

We believe that approach (3) achieves a proper balance of openness of enquiry with not making it easy for potential or further non-disclosure.

11. The Solicitor Continuing to Act

In certain circumstances of non or misleading disclosure, the solicitor should not continue to act.

(i)   The client says: 'I will not disclose anything at all'. After the client has been advised of the costs and inference sanctions of the court, the solicitor can continue to act, provided he is not privy to any information which is not disclosed or is misleadingly disclosed.

(ii)   The client says: 'I have asset X but I require you not to disclose it'. The solicitor cannot continue to act for this non-disclosing client because the solicitor is in breach of duty to the court not to mislead it.

(iii)   After initial disclosure, the client admits to the existence of additional assets etc. If disclosure is then given, the solicitor can continue to act. If the client refuses to disclose, the solicitor cannot continue to act.

It is necessary in some cases to consider the benefit to the case in continuing to act eg of any ongoing relationship with the client, if there is a realistic prospect of the client thus being encouraged to give early and/or full disclosure. The solicitor may then be able to continue to act provided his personal integrity was not compromised, he did not mislead the court or the other parties' representatives in any way and he genuinely believed he would be a good persuasive influence over the client.

Good Practice

We are satisfied that the importance of disclosure, and the mischief created by non/misleading disclosure requires that serious action is called for, for example by the solicitor assessing at an early stage whether he should continue to act. This threat may cause some clients to agree to give disclosure.

12. Other Statutory Provisions

There are a number of other statutory provisions relevant to self-help action such as trespass, s 1 Criminal Damage Act 1971 which establishes the offence of without lawful excuse destroying or damaging property belonging to another, Theft Act 1968, s 9 which establishes the offence of burglary, Unlawful retention of documents and Obtaining information by deception.

13. Multiplicity of Actions

It is possible for separate proceedings to be commenced, perhaps based on matters referred to above.

Good Practice

1.   Although actions for damages or other civil remedies may lie as a result of one party's self-help actions vis à vis the other (or for other reasons), the family courts discourage multiplicity of actions. Constantly family court judges say that their discretion is wide enough to encompass such other actions' remedies. Instead such other proceedings can, in some cases, add to costs, amount of court documents and delay matters, yet not vary the final outcome.

2.   There is nothing to prevent a separate action being taken, so it is properly pleaded, and then being consolidated with the family law proceedings. However the outcome of the 'separate action' will be in the context of the overall ancillary relief settlement.

3.   If a party contemplates taking such proceedings after the divorce action is over, there is a duty to disclose it as, if it were successful, it would represent a material resource/liability that the family court should take into account.

4.   Where actions involve third parties, even third parties who are not members of the parties' family, there may still be a consolidation with the family proceedings. This includes cases where the nexus with the divorce seems slight but simply due to some courts' wish to avoid multiplicity of actions and issues. Instead interpleader etc applications can be made.

Note:
1.   This good practice guidance does not and cannot affect any obligations in law, specific court orders or rules of professional conduct.
2.   Good practice guidance can inevitably only deal with generality of situations. It cannot be an absolute rule. The special facts of any particular case may justify and/or require a solicitor to depart from these guide-lines.
3.   It is the view of the SFLA Good Practice Committee that this guidance applies to all family law cases for the better conduct and approach to resolution of family breakdown issues, and not just to cases between SFLA members.

SFLA GOOD PRACTICE COMMITTEE
January 1996

David Hodson (chairman)
Alastair Babbington
Wendy Boyce
John Cornwell
Deborah Leask
David Newton
James Pirrie
Jane Simpson
Beth Wilkins

Summary of Information Available in Respect of Offshore Companies

	Bahamas	British Virgin Islands	Gibraltar	Isle of Man	Jersey
Date incorporated	✔	✔	✔	✔	✔
Company number	✔	✔	✔	✔	✔
Changes of name	✔	✔	✔	✔	✔
Registered office address	✔	✔	✔	✔	✔
Principal objects and powers	✔	✔	✔	✔	✔
Authorised capital	✔	✔	✔	✔	✔
Issued capital			✔	✔	✔
Shareholders	see note 1	see note 1	✔	✔	✔
Directors	see note 1	see note 1	✔	✔	see note 2
Mortgages/charges	see note 1	see note 1	✔	✔	
Accounts				see note 2	see note 2
Any dissolution, winding up	✔	✔	✔	✔	✔

Notes
1. There is no legal requirement for offshore companies to file this information.
2. Only available on public companies.

Practice Direction: Case Management
[1995] 1 FLR 456

Greater court control over preparation for, and conduct of, hearings – Cost consequences of cases not being conducted economically

(1)   The importance of reducing the cost and delay of civil litigation makes it necessary for the court to assert greater control over the preparation for and conduct of hearings than has hitherto been customary. Failure by practitioners to conduct cases economically will be visited by appropriate orders for costs, including wasted costs orders.

(2)   The court will accordingly exercise its discretion to limit:

   (a)   discovery;
   (b)   the length of opening and closing oral submissions;
   (c)   the time allowed for the examination and cross-examination of witnesses;
   (d)   the issues on which it wishes to be addressed;
   (e)   reading aloud from documents and authorities.

(3)   Unless otherwise ordered, every witness statement or affidavit shall stand as the evidence-in-chief of the witness concerned. The substance of the evidence which a party intends to adduce at the hearing must be sufficiently detailed, but without prolixity; it must be confined to material matters of fact, not (except in the case of the evidence of professional witnesses) of opinion; and if hearsay evidence is to be adduced, the source of the information must be declared or good reason given for not doing so.

(4)   It is a duty owed to the court both by the parties and by their legal representatives to give full and frank disclosure in ancillary relief applications and also in all matters in respect of children. The parties and their advisers must also use their best endeavours:

   (a)   to confine the issues and the evidence called to what is reasonably considered to be essential for the proper presentation of their case;
   (b)   to reduce or eliminate issues for expert evidence;
   (c)   in advance of the hearing to agree which are the issues or the main issues.

(5)   Unless the nature of the hearing makes it unnecessary and in the absence of specific directions, bundles should be agreed and prepared for use by the Court, the parties and the witnesses and shall be in A4 format where possible,

suitably secured. The bundles for use by the court shall be lodged with the court (the Clerk of the Rules in matters in the Royal Courts of Justice, London) at least 2 clear days before the hearing. Each bundle should be paginated, indexed, wholly legible, and arranged chronologically. Where documents are copied unnecessarily or bundled incompetently the cost will be disallowed.

(6)   In cases estimated to last for 5 days or more and in which no pre-trial review has been ordered, application should be made for a pre-trial review. It should, when practicable, be listed at least 3 weeks before the hearing and be conducted by the judge or district judge before whom the case is to be heard and should be attended by the advocates who are to represent the parties at the hearing. Whenever possible, all statements of evidence and all reports should be filed before the date of the review and in good time for them to have been considered by all parties.

(7)   Whenever practicable and in any matter estimated to last 5 days or more, each party should, not less than 2 clear days before the hearing, lodge with the court, or the Clerk of the Rules in matters in the Royal Courts of Justice, in London, and deliver to other parties, a chronology and a skeleton argument concisely summarising that party's submissions in relation to each of the issues, and citing the main authorities relied upon. It is important that skeleton arguments should be brief.

(8)   In advance of the hearing upon request, and otherwise in the course of their opening, parties should be prepared to furnish the court, if there is no core bundle, with a list of documents essential for a proper understanding of the case.

(9)   The opening speech should be succinct. At its conclusion, other parties may be invited briefly to amplify their skeleton arguments. In a heavy case the court may in conjunction with final speeches require written submissions, including the findings of fact for which each party contends.

(10)   This Practice Direction which follows the directions handed down by the Lord Chief Justice and the Vice-Chancellor to apply in the Queen's Bench and Chancery Divisions, shall apply to all family proceedings in the High Court and in all care centres, family hearing centres and divorce county courts.

(11)   Issued with the concurrence of the Lord Chancellor.

31 January 1995   SIR STEPHEN BROWN
                                                              President

Precedent

ORDER UNDER THE BANKERS' BOOKS EVIDENCE ACT 1879, FOR INSPECTION AND COPYING OF BANK BOOKS AND RECORDS

IN THE ANYTOWN COUNTY COURT   CASE NO.

BETWEEN: JACK HILL   PETITIONER
                              and
        JILL HILL   RESPONDENT

BEFORE DISTRICT JUDGE WHITE
The 1st day of December 1994

Upon hearing the Solicitor for the Petitioner and upon the Respondent and the Britannic Bank having been served and not appearing,
And pursuant to section 7 of the Bankers' Books Evidence Act 1879,

IT IS ORDERED that Horatio V. Honest the Solicitor for the Petitioner shall be at liberty to inspect and take copies of certain books and records of the Britannic Bank namely the record of the payees of the following cheques drawn by the Respondent on his account number 987654321:
cheques numbers 001234, 001237, 001240 and 001246.
Such inspection and taking copies shall be permitted within seven days of service of the Order upon the said Bank.

AND IT IS FURTHER ORDERED that the respondent shall pay the costs of and incidental to this application.

Example of Annual Report and Financial Statements for a Private Limited Company

FAVOURITE FASHIONS LIMITED

**Annual report and financial statements
for the year ended 31 March 2001**

CONTENTS

FAVOURITE FASHIONS LIMITED

DIRECTORS' REPORT FOR THE YEAR ENDED 31 MARCH 2001

The directors present their report and the audited financial statements of the company for the year ended 31 March 2001.

Principal activities

The principal activity of the company continues to be the manufacture of exclusive ladies' fashions.

Review of business and future developments

During the year to 31 March 2002 the company intends to expand into men's fashions.

Results and dividends

The company's profit for the financial year is £202,990 (2000: £396,473). A final dividend of 300p (2000: 300p) per ordinary share amounting to £15,000 (2000: £15,000) is proposed and, if approved, will be paid on 1 February 2001.

Directors

The directors who held office during the year and their interest in the ordinary share capital of the company are given below:

	2001	2000
	£	£
Charles Shackleton	5,000*	5,000*
Peter Ward	–	–
Douglas Davidson	–	–
Helen Meltzer	–	–
David Doran	–	–
	£5,000	£5,000

* Includes 1,000 shares held by Mrs Charles Shackleton

Statement of Directors' Responsibilities

Company law requires the directors to prepare financial statements for each financial year that give a true and fair view of the state of affairs of the company and of the profit or loss of the company for that period.

The directors confirm that suitable accounting policies have been used and applied consistently with the exception of the changes arising on the adoption of new accounting standards in the year as explained on page 10 under Note 1

Page 2

FAVOURITE FASHIONS LIMITED

'Accounting policies'. They also confirm that reasonable and prudent judgements and estimates have been made in preparing the financial statements for the year ended 31 March 2001 and that applicable accounting standards have been followed.

The directors are responsible for keeping proper accounting records that disclose with reasonable accuracy at any time the financial position of the company and enable them to ensure that the financial statements comply with the Companies Act 1985. They are also responsible for safeguarding the assets of the company and hence for taking reasonable steps for the prevention and detection of fraud and other irregularities.

Auditors

The auditors, Tickett and Sine, have indicated their willingness to continue in office, and a resolution concerning their reappointment will be proposed at the Annual General Meeting.

By order of the Board

John Brown

SECRETARY

26 June 2001

FAVOURITE FASHIONS LIMITED

AUDITORS' REPORT TO THE MEMBERS OF FAVOURITE FASHIONS LIMITED

We have audited the financial statements on pages 6 to 14.

Respective responsibilities of directors and auditors

The directors are responsible for preparing the annual report including, as described on page 2, preparing the financial statements in accordance with applicable United Kingdom accounting standards. Our responsibilities, as independent auditors, are established in the United Kingdom by statute, the Auditing Practices Board and our profession's ethical guidance.

We report to you our opinion as to whether the financial statements give a true and fair view and are properly prepared in accordance with the United Kingdom Companies Act. We also report to you if, in our opinion, the directors' report is not consistent with the financial statements, if the company has not kept proper accounting records, if we have not received all the information and explanations we require for our audit, or if information specified by law regarding directors' remuneration and transactions is not disclosed.

We read the other information contained in the annual report and consider the implications for our report if we become aware of any apparent misstatements or material inconsistencies with the financial statements.

Basis of audit opinion

We conducted our audit in accordance with the Auditing Standards issued by the Auditing Practices Board. An audit includes examination, on a test basis, of evidence relevant to the amounts and disclosures in the financial statements. It also includes an assessment of the significant estimates and judgements made by the directors in the preparation of the financial statements, and of whether the accounting policies are appropriate to the company's circumstances, consistently applied and adequately disclosed.

We planned and performed our audit so as to obtain all the information and explanations which we considered necessary in order to provide us with sufficient evidence to give reasonable assurance that the financial statements are free from material misstatement, whether caused by fraud or other irregularity or error. In forming our opinion we also evaluated the overall adequacy of the presentation of information in the financial statements.

FAVOURITE FASHIONS LIMITED

Opinion

In our opinion the financial statements give a true and fair view of the state of the company's affairs at 31 March 2001 and of its profit for the year ended and have been properly prepared in accordance with the Companies Act 1985.

Tickett and Sine

Chartered Accountants and Registered Auditor

26 June 2001

FAVOURITE FASHIONS LIMITED

Profit and Loss Account for the year ended 31 March 2001

	Note	2001		2000	
		£		£	
Turnover – continuing operations		6,963,245		6,843,920	
Cost of sales		(5,810,432)		(5,468,624)	
Gross profit		1,152,813		1,375,296	
Distribution costs		259,160		261,612	
Administrative expenses		501,920		415,694	
		(761,080)		(677,306)	
Operating profit – continuing operations	3	391,733		697,990	
Interest receivable		425		401	
		392,158		698,391	
Interest payable	6	(24,950)		(24,950)	
Profit on ordinary activities before taxation		367,208		673,441	
Taxation on profits on ordinary activities	7	(149,218)		(261,968)	
Profit on ordinary activities after taxation		217,990		411,473	
Dividends	8	(15,000)		(15,000)	
Retained profit for the financial year		202,990		396,473	
Retained profit brought forward		1,440,394		1,043,921	
		1,643,384		1,440,394	
Retained (loss)/profit carried forward		£1,643,384		£1,440,394	

The company has no recognised gains and losses other than the profit above and therefore no separate statement of total recognised gains and losses has been presented.

There is no difference between the profit on ordinary activities before taxation and the retained profit for the year stated above and their historical cost equivalents.

FAVOURITE FASHIONS LIMITED

Balance sheet at 31 March 2001

	Note	2001	2000
		£	£
Fixed assets			
Tangible assets	9	830,224	714,426
Current assets			
Stocks and work in progress	10	829,201	986,432
Debtors	11	1,006,612	1,025,719
Cash at bank and in hand		482,103	263,459
		2,317,916	2,275,610
Creditors:			
Amounts falling due within one year	12	(1,124,200)	(1,245,930)
Provisions for liabilities and charges	13	(125,556)	(48,712)
Net current assets		1,068,160	980,968
Total assets less current liabilities		1,898,384	1,695,394
Creditors:			
Amounts falling due after more than one year	14	(250,000)	(250,000)
		£1,648,384	£1,445,394
Capital and reserves			
Called up share capital	15	5,000	5,000
Profit and Loss Account		1,643,384	1,440,394
Total equity shareholders' funds		£1,648,384	£1,445,394

C Shackleton   )

H Meltzer   )   Directors   Date: 26 June 2001

FAVOURITE FASHIONS LIMITED

Cash flow statement for the year ended 31 March 2001

	£	£
Net cash inflow from operating activities		725,337
Returns on investments and servicing of finance		
Interest received	425	
Interest paid	(24,950)	
Net cash outflow from returns on investments and servicing of finance		(24,525)
Taxation		
UK Corporation tax paid	(261,968)	
Tax paid		(261,968)
Capital expenditure and financial investment		
Purchase of tangible fixed assets	(220,700)	
Sale of plant and machinery	15,500	
Net cash outflow for capital expenditure and financial investment		(205,200)
Equity dividends paid to shareholders		(15,000)
Net cash inflow before financing		218,644
Financing		–
Increase in net cash		218,644

FAVOURITE FASHIONS LIMITED

Notes to the cash flow statement

1 Reconciliation of operating profit to net cash flow from operating activities

	£
Operating profit	391,733
Depreciation charges	89,402
Profit on sale of tangible fixed assets	–
Decrease in stocks	157,231
Decrease in debtors	19,107
Decrease in creditors	(8,980)
Increase in provisions and charges	76,844
Net cash inflow from operating activities	725,337

2 Analysis of changes in cash and cash equivalents during the year

	£
Balance at 31 March 2000	263,459
Net cash flow before adjustments for foreign exchange rates	218,644
Effect of foreign exchange rates	–
Balance at 31 March 2001	482,103

3 Analysis of changes in financing during the year

	Share capital	Long term loan
	£	£
Financing at 31 March 2000	5,000	250,000
Cash flow from financing	–	–
Financing at 31 March 2001	5,000	250,000

FAVOURITE FASHIONS LIMITED

Notes to the financial statements for the year ended 31 March 2001

1 Accounting policies

These financial statements are prepared under the historical cost convention, the accounting policies set out below and in accordance with applicable accounting standards.

Turnover

Turnover represents sales to outside customers at invoiced amounts less Value Added Tax.

Tangible fixed assets

The cost of tangible assets is their purchase cost, together with any incidental costs of acquisition.

Depreciation is calculated so as to write off the cost of tangible fixed assets, less their estimated residual values, on a straight-line basis over the expected useful economic lives of the assets concerned. The principal annual rates used for this purpose are:

> Freehold property – 1% pa
> Fixtures and fittings – 10% pa
> Plant, machinery and vehicles – 10% pa

Stocks

Stocks and Work in Progress are stated at the lower of cost and net realisable value. In general, cost is determined in a first in first out basis and includes transport and handling costs. Net realisable value is based on estimated selling price less further costs to completion.

Deferred taxation

Provision is made for deferred taxation, using the liability method, on all material timing differences to the extent that it is probable that a liability or asset will crystallise.

Pensions

During the year the company operated a defined contribution scheme on behalf of certain of its employees. The charge against profits is the amount of contributions payable to the pension scheme in respect of the accounting period.

FAVOURITE FASHIONS LIMITED

2 Segmental reporting

Turnover consists entirely of sales made in the United Kingdom.

3 Operating profit

Operating profit is stated after charging

	2001	2000
	£	£
Wages and salaries	1,077,586	1,024,994
Social Security costs	190,162	183,056
Staff costs	1,267,748	1,208,050
Depreciation of tangible fixed assets	89,402	138,000
Auditors' remuneration	19,000	18,000

4 Directors' emoluments

	2001	2000
	£	£
Aggregate emoluments	160,000	149,000
Company pension contributions to the defined contribution scheme	15,000	31,000
	£175,000	£180,000

Retirement benefits are accruing to five (2000: five) directors under the company's defined contribution scheme.

5 Employee information

The average monthly number of persons (including executive directors) employed by the company during the year was as follows:

	2001	2000
	£	£
Manufacturing	89	90
Selling and distribution	40	39
Administration	13	12
	142	141

FAVOURITE FASHIONS LIMITED

6   Interest payable and similar charges

	2001	2000
	£	£
Interest payable on bank loans wholly repayable within five years	24,950	24,950

7   Tax on profits from ordinary activities

	2001	2000
	£	£
UK corporation tax at 30% (2000: 30.25%)	149,218	261,968

8   Dividends

	2001	2000
	£	£
Equity – Ordinary		
Final proposed: 300p (2000: 300p) per £1 share	15,000	15,000
	15,000	15,000

FAVOURITE FASHIONS LIMITED

9 Tangible fixed assets

Group	Freehold property	Plant machinery and vehicles	Fixtures and fittings	Total
	£	£	£	£
Cost or valuation:				
At 1 April 2000	350,000	435,600	396,420	1,182,020
Additions	–	60,000	160,700	220,700
Disposals	–	(15,500)	–	(15,500)
	£350,000	£480,100	£557,120	£1,387,220
Depreciation:				
At 1 April 2000	28,000	249,600	189,994	467,594
Provided during the year	3,500	43,760	42,142	89,402
At 31 March 2001	£31,500	£293,360	£232,136	£556,996
Net book value:				
At 1 April 2000	£322,000	£186,000	£206,426	£714,426
At 31 March 2001	£318,500	£186,740	£324,984	£830,224

10 Stocks

	2001	2000
	£	£
Work in progress	523,160	562,204
Finished goods and goods for resale	306,041	424,228
	£829,201	£986,432

11 Debtors

	2001	2000
	£	£
Trade debtors	942,581	1,007,028
Prepayments and accrued income	64,031	18,691
	£1,006,612	£1,025,719

Page 13

FAVOURITE FASHIONS LIMITED

12   Creditors: amounts falling due within one year

	2001	2000
	£	£
Director's current account	53,000	40,000
Trade creditors	902,612	923,014
Taxation and social security	149,218	261,968
Accruals and deferred income	4,370	5,948
Proposed dividend	15,000	15,000
	£1,124,200	£1,245,930

13   Provisions for liabilities and charges

	Balance at 1.4.00	Movement in year	Balance at 31.3.01
Advertising	5,000	80,000	85,000
Repairs and maintenance	43,712	(3,156)	40,556
	£48,712	£76,844	£125,556

14   Creditors – amounts falling due after more than one year

	2001	2000
	£	£
Bank loan account	250,000	250,000

The loan is repayable on 1 April 2003

15   Called up share capital

	2001	2000
	£	£
Authorised, allotted and fully paid up	5,000	5,000
	£5,000	£5,000

For the purposes of this Appendix, a reconciliation of movements in shareholders' funds, as required by Financial Reporting Standard 2, and reconciliations of the movement in net debt, as required by Financial Reporting Standard 1, have not been prepared.

FAVOURITE FASHIONS LIMITED

Detailed trading profit and loss account for the year ended 31 March 2001

	£	2001 £	£	2000 £
Turnover		6,963,245		6,843,920
Less: cost of sales				
Opening stock	986,432		855,000	
Purchases	4,593,519		4,554,453	
Manufacturing wages/NI	1,014,981		976,603	
Depreciation	44,701		69,000	
Less: closing stock	(829,201)		(986,432)	
		(5,810,432)		(5,468,624)
Gross profit		1,152,813		1,375,296
Less: distribution costs				
Carriage in	15,336		19,379	
Carriage outwards	15,409		20,850	
Depreciation	22,351		34,500	
Petrol and diesel	43,850		41,725	
Distribution wages/NI	162,214		145,158	
		(259,160)		(261,612)
Less: administrative costs				
Entertaining	34,533		12,320	
Administrative salaries/NI	90,553		86,289	
Rates	18,514		15,232	
Light and heat	5,129		4,390	
Bad debts	3,598		2,560	
Directors' salaries	160,000		149,000	
National insurance	14,050		14,020	
Directors' pensions	15,000		31,000	
Depreciation	22,350		34,500	
Telephone and stationery	7,046		6,387	
Repairs and renewals	1,196		1,163	
Auditors' remuneration	19,000		18,000	
Travel and advertising	82,423		22,203	
Sundry	28,528		18,630	
		(501,920)		(415,694)
		391,733		697,990

Page 15

INDEX

References are to paragraph numbers, references in *italic* are to Appendix page numbers.